LIMINAL THINKING

Create the Change You Want by Changing the Way You Think

DAVE GRAY

TWO WAVES
BOOKS

TWO WAVES BOOKS
BROOKLYN, NY, USA

Liminal Thinking
Create the Change You Want by Changing the Way You Think
By Dave Gray

Two Waves Books
an Imprint of Rosenfeld Media, LLC
457 Third Street, #4R
Brooklyn, New York
11215 USA

On the Web: twowavesbooks.com
Please send errors to: errata@twowavesbooks.com

Publisher: Louis Rosenfeld
Managing Editor: Marta Justak
Illustrations: Dave Gray
Interior Layout Tech: Danielle Foster
Cover and Interior Design: The Heads of State
Indexer: Sharon Shock
Proofreader: Chuck Hutchinson

ISBN: 1-933820-46-2
ISBN-13: 978-1-933820-46-0
LCCN: 2016938554

Printed and bound in the United States of America

Dedicated to Kurt Hanks,
without whom this book would not exist

Advance Praise for *Liminal Thinking*

"Ever since I found out about *Liminal Thinking*, I keep thinking of it at strange times, in-between times, surprising times. I keep thinking, wouldn't it be great if this person were exposed to Dave's book, or here's what I'd like to say right now, it's right here in Dave's book, or I feel a need to reread this part of Dave's book. I take these messages as signs that Dave's book is a book we all need, even if we don't all know it yet. I can't wait for everyone to discover it."

—*Cynthia Kurtz, researcher, software developer, consultant, and author,* Working with Stories

"*Liminal Thinking* is yet another compelling-to-read, mind-expanding book by Dave Gray. In an era of accelerating change, uncertainty, and opportunity, readers in all walks of life will benefit from the visual thinking insights of this tremendous book."

—*Jonathan H. King, Head of Cloud Strategy, Ericsson & Visiting Scholar, Washington University School of Law*

"The universe becomes clearer through Dave Gray's eyes."

—*Robin Uchida*

"In a time of increasing complexity and change, Dave Gray's *Liminal Thinking* provides a much-needed blueprint to help us clarify our own thinking, make connections with others, and communicate our ideas powerfully, in a way that is both deeply human and profoundly impactful."

—*Lisa Kay Solomon, Co-Author,* Moments of Impact: How to Design Strategic Conversations That Accelerate Change

"Liminal Thinking is an invaluable leadership tool, for the quality of our thinking determines how we connect, lead and generate impact."

—*Carlos Salum, Salum International*

"Change, it's inevitable, and it will happen whether you're proactive or reactive. Becoming an effective agent for change is invaluable. In *Liminal Thinking*, Dave Gray nails it! For almost two decades, I've tried, often unsuccessfully, to teach the beliefs and fundamental change principles that David explains so simply and powerfully. The Rabbis of the Talmud had a saying: 'jealousy between scholars increases wisdom.' I am jealous. Do yourself a favor, buy this short book and finish reading it immediately."

—*Jeffrey Eisenberg, Author of NY Times Best Sellers* Call to Action *and* Waiting for Your Cat to Bark?"

"*Liminal Thinking* is an accessible and engaging foray into a dark recess of organizational development that opens up many possibilities for profound change at the levels of self, organization, and society. Entering the liminal zone requires you to confront scary ideas, entertain wild beliefs, and accept personal risk. But liminal thinking is exactly what is required if we are to make progress on today's most intractable challenges."

—*Alex Ryan, Senior Systems Design Manager, Government of Alberta*

"I've just sat and demolished, devoured, gorged myself on the book. It's just brilliant. Rarely do you read a book nowadays that feels so expertly, artfully designed to enlighten with every continuing page. Story by story, Dave demonstrates a new way to think about thinking, and gives you simple ways to put it into practice for yourself. Each chapter is a subtle jab to the edifice of 20th century practices, and just wait until you get to that left hook. Dave Gray is the Marvin Hagler of the mind."

—*John Willshire, Strategic Designer and Founder, Smithery*

"The book is absolutely stunning! It reminds me of sand mandalas constructed by monks. Each sentence in the book is patently and blatantly obvious. The text and figures are eminently accessible to any adult who can read. Like a mandala, there is a miraculous-like synergy and beauty that emerges when viewed in its entirety."

—*Richard Gray, Biomedical Engineer, U.S. Food and Drug Administration*

"This is an important and deeply useful book for both individuals and organizations. Using simple and intuitive illustrated frameworks, and clearly explained premises and principles, Dave Gray makes some underlying truths about human nature more accessible and explicit.

"One important contribution the book makes is the title itself. By helping to coin the word *liminal thinking*, Gray is giving a name to a powerful thing.

"This kind of thinking is crucial in the fast-paced, high-pressure business world we all now operate in. And, even more fundamentally, in a world that's facing some very real problems for humanity.

"On its face, this is a business book. However, this is the kind of business book that makes you realize that businesses are just a bunch of humans working together. Because the book seeks to uncover the underlying dynamics of how people think, communicate, and make decisions, its insights are useful in many spheres and circumstances."

—*Adam Menter, Learning Strategist, Autodesk*

"I can't believe you actually finish your books."

—*Karl Gude, School of Journalism, Michigan State University*

"Life is complicated. There are no quick answers to your biggest problems. How are we to make any progress? Train your brain, and become a mental gymnast! Let Dave Gray and *Liminal Thinking* be your guide."

—*Chris Reimer, Author of* Happywork

"Dave Gray has taken the brilliantly simple germ of an idea (how to think across the borders of belief) and written it into a potent virus. Dave's timing couldn't be better. As the world slips again into splintered conflicts of belief, I hope and pray his virus spreads."

—*Dan Roam, author of* The Back of the Napkin

"*Liminal thinking*, two words that hold in them such a kind energy to enact powerful change. I read Dave's book right when I needed it most. I feel many of us will always feel that way picking up this book time and again. It is a light and easy-to-access volume we can return to over and over when we need to nourish ourselves, our values, and our vision to enact change to make a better world. Simple language, clear organization of complex concepts, and ease of accessibility show that Dave is really a master and precise wielder of his art, the art of making the complex simple and the simple compelling."

—*Alicia Dudek, Lead Design Ethnographer and Innovator, Deloitte Australia*

"This book will unlock the magical and often hidden parts behind change. You will have the tools to think differently and to help others think differently. Dave has found yet another way to simplify the understanding of the map for the key journeys for evolving human potential."

—*Mike Hruska, President & CEO, Problem Solutions*

"*Liminal Thinking* is a book about how to be mentally healthy, how to be present, and how to be a positive force in the world. But more simply, and more importantly, it's a book about how to be."

—*Daniel H. Pink, author of* Drive *and* To Sell Is Human

Contents at a Glance

Contents and Executive Summary

Liminal Thinking is the art of creating change by understanding, shaping, and reframing beliefs.

These six principles constitute a theory of beliefs: how they come into being, why they are necessary, how they are reinforced over time, and why people cling to their beliefs, even when they are incomplete, obsolete, or invalid. They are beliefs about beliefs.

Beliefs seem like perfect representations of the world, but, in fact, they are imperfect models for navigating a complex, multidimensional, unknowable reality.

Beliefs are constructed hierarchically, using theories and judgments, which are based on selected facts and personal, subjective experiences.

Foreword

It's necessary if you've gotten this far in Dave's newest book—and I say *newest* because he is prolific and his energy pervades his passion about thinking and understanding—it is necessary to read his definition of the word *liminal*, a word that I had never heard before he asked me to do this foreword, but I'm envious and jealous that he thought it up as the name of a book.

In fact, in the off chance that he's not going to use it in the beginning of his book, I'll reproduce his definition here as the beginning of my introduction to his many words:

"What is liminal thinking? *Liminal* is a word that means boundary, doorway, portal. Not this or that, not the old way or the new way, but neither and both. A state of ambiguity or disorientation that precedes a breakthrough to a new kind of thinking. The space between. Liminal thinking is a kind of psychological agility that enables you to successfully navigate these times of transition. It involves the ability to read your own beliefs and needs; the ability to read others' beliefs and needs; and the habit of continually evaluating, validating, and changing beliefs in order to better meet needs."

We both recognize that the look of things, the name of things, forms the doorknob to the door and belongs in this great villa of learning and understanding that pervades mankind. Each of us resides in some strange side chapel, which we poke our nose out of every once in a while, prod the rest of them, and invite them over into our little alcove for our odd interpretation and individual definitions of how to join us in a more interesting, more productive, and more understanding life.

This is certainly a book to be read because it is like being with Dave himself, filled with the energy of his conviction, his whole belief system about how to get through our life of thinking and making sense, asking questions, exploring our alternatives, and in a conversational way, with Super Glue attached, putting it all together in an amalgam of a story.

Boy, does Dave do it well, and he seems to do it effortlessly. He can produce one of these babies in one-tenth the time it would take me. Dave is formidable physically, so it's accurate for me to say that when I'm in his presence, I look up to him and he looks down on me.

When we're sitting, I think we're more equal and very much in the same street, neighborhood, village, town, city, county, and country. In the best sense of the word, this is popularization of the obvious, of the space between things, of seeing things you've always seen but never seen and pulling them into your own personal library, for getting through the morass, the flotsam and jetsam of all the stuff that's around us.

He's on my short list of a very short list of kindred spirits. I wish him well. And you would be wise to get past my prattle and read his book.

—Richard Saul Wurman
Newport, R.I.
10 August 2015

Preface

How This Book Came to Be

A new type of thinking is essential if mankind is to survive and move toward higher levels.

—Albert Einstein

Some years ago, I came across a book that had inspired me as a high school student. The book was called *Rapid Viz: A New Method for the Rapid Visualization of Ideas* by Kurt Hanks. It was the first time I had ever seen someone articulate the idea of drawing as thinking, which since then has become a central theme of my life and work.

The book taught me that drawing is not just a means for illustrating ideas that already exist, but also a medium for exploration, investigation, thinking, and discovery.

The book sat on my shelf for many years, but one day I opened it again, and I was happy to find that it was still as clear, fresh, and compelling as the book I had first opened 20 years earlier.

On a whim, I searched for the author on Google, found his website, and sent him a message through his contact form. The note was quite short:

> Hi Kurt,
>
> Just a note to say that your books have been a great inspiration to me – thanks!
>
> Dave

To my surprise and delight, he answered me, which started a dialogue, which became a friendship, which ultimately led directly to the book you're holding in your hands right now.

What I know now, but didn't know then, was that Kurt is far more than a visual thinker and designer. He is something that I didn't really have a name for at the time, but which I now call a *liminal thinker*. In some ways, he is like a designer or an architect; in other ways, like a psychologist. His art is helping people break down, examine, explore, analyze, and reconfigure their beliefs. More often than not, this process leads to profound change.

One of the reasons he is so good at this is his bedside manner. He is a warm and caring person and one of the best listeners I know. He does not judge.

What I learned from Kurt is that beliefs are often the main things standing in the way of change, not only for individuals, but also for teams, families, organizations, nations, and even the world as a whole.

It took me some years to absorb Kurt's philosophy, and even longer to learn how to apply it to my work as a leader and management consultant. I'm still learning new things from him all the time.

My early interest in design was sparked by Kurt's work, many years ago, so I suppose I shouldn't be surprised that years later, he would inspire me again and spark a renaissance in my life and work.

As a consultant, I would try some of Kurt's ideas on a large project and find that they succeeded beyond my wildest dreams. The more I worked in the world of organizations and transformation, the more I kept coming back to Kurt's fundamental premise:

> We construct our beliefs, mostly unconsciously, and thereafter they hold us captive. They can help us focus and make us more effective, but sadly, they also can limit us: they blind us to possibility and subject us to fog, fear, and doubt.

Kurt and I have agreed, in the spirit of friendship and in the interest of growing the exciting discipline that we have started to call *liminal thinking*, to steal liberally from each other.

Nevertheless, I would like to acknowledge him as the source for many of the ideas you will find in this book. Kurt has been working with hearts, minds, and beliefs for many years.

This book is dedicated to Kurt Hanks, my friend and mentor.

Introduction

What Is Liminal Thinking?

Once you see the boundaries of your environment, they are no longer the boundaries of your environment.

—Marshall McLuhan

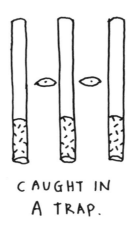

C AUGHT IN
A TRAP.

Have you ever had a moment that changed your life forever?

When I was 29 years old, I desperately wanted to quit smoking, but I didn't believe I could do it. I felt like I was caught in a trap. I didn't want to smoke anymore, but I didn't think I could quit. I had tried before and failed.

Then one day, I was sick with a chest cold. I was so addicted that even though I was sick and coughing, I didn't stop smoking, not even for a day. As I sat there, in my bathrobe, coughing and smoking, I pictured myself as an old man, wheezing, unable to catch my breath, and feeling that way all the time, not just when I was sick.

That day, impulsively, I quit. It wasn't easy, but to my own surprise, I stuck with it and haven't had a cigarette for more than 20 years.

That in itself was a huge change. But it was accompanied by a deeper change. I realized that if I could quit smoking—something I had thought was impossible—then I was capable of a lot more. The confidence and courage I gained by quitting smoking led me to change my life in far more profound ways. Within the next few months, I ended my relationship with my girlfriend, quit my job, changed industries, moved across the country, and started my own business.

My whole perspective had changed. And that shift in perspective changed my life.

A NEW WAY OF
SEEING OPENS
DOORS TO NEW
POSSIBILITIES

Have you had moments like this in your life, when you suddenly saw things in a new and different way?

A new way of seeing the world—and yourself—opens the door to change and growth.

You can cultivate a way of thinking and being that will allow you to have these breakthrough insights more often. Through that new way of thinking, you will be able to guide others to similar mind shifts that will give them the power to transform their lives. This way of thinking is a practice you can use to find and create new doorways to possibilities, doorways that are invisible to others.

I call this practice *liminal thinking.*

The word *liminal* comes from the Latin root *limen*, which means *threshold*.

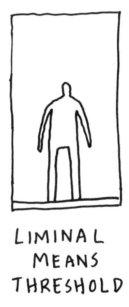

LIMINAL
MEANS
THRESHOLD

A threshold is a border, a boundary, or an edge. It is a marginal, in-between space that defines two things, while at the same time being neither one nor the other.

Most boundaries are convenient fictions. What divides the people who are "on" a team from those who are not? What separates one company department or division from another, or an employee from a customer? Boundaries give life structure, which makes us comfortable. But they can also be shifted, rethought, reframed, and reorganized.

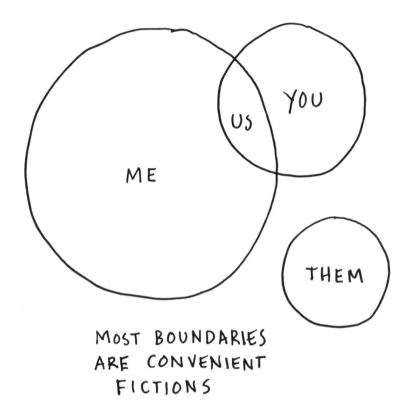

MOST BOUNDARIES
ARE CONVENIENT
FICTIONS

Change happens at the boundaries of things: the boundary between the known and the unknown, the familiar and the different, between the old way and the new way, the past and the future.

Some roles are liminal in nature. A coach, for example, is part of the team and not part of the team at the same time. A consultant works in a company, without being part of the company. A therapist has access to the deepest emotions of family life, while not being part of the family. A teacher is part of the class and not part of the class.

These are liminal roles because they are associated with growth and change, which involve breaking, shifting, or otherwise transcending boundaries

You have liminal moments every day, when you are just waking up and when you are just falling asleep. You usually don't notice these liminal moments, but they are valuable sources of creativity and insight. Ever have a good idea in the shower or in the middle of the night? That happened because your mind was relaxed and open to possibilities.[1]

The idea behind liminal thinking is that there are thresholds, doors of opportunity, around you, all the time. Most of them are invisible to you, because you are focusing on other things. But they are there, they are real, and they offer incredible potential for growth and change. Tuning your mind to liminal thinking will help you see opportunities that others will be unable to see or even imagine. It's a kind of psychological agility that enables you to create change where others cannot.

You don't need any formal authority, budget, or official sanction to be successful at liminal thinking. All that's required is one person with a desire to create change.

Liminal thinking, like any other craft, requires a deep understanding of its materials.

If you are a carpenter, you must understand your tools, the theories behind them, and how to use them. Whether you are a doctor, a mechanic, a lawyer, or a gardener, the same rule applies.

---

1. For more on this fascinating boundary between sleep and wakefulness, just look up "hypnagogia."

No matter what you do, the better and more deeply you can understand your materials, the more possibilities you will be able to create.

In liminal thinking, the most important material to understand is belief.

BELIEF IS A MATERIAL

Liminal thinking is the art of creating change by understanding, shaping, and reframing beliefs.

EXERCISE

Think of something in your life that you see as problematic, but that you don't think will ever change. Consider the connection between how you see the problem and how you see yourself. What if you saw yourself differently? If you were the kind of person who could change this situation, what would you be like? How would you act?

How Beliefs Shape Everything

The following six principles constitute a theory of beliefs: how they come into being, why they are necessary, how they are reinforced over time, and why people cling to their beliefs, even when they are incomplete, obsolete, or invalid. They are beliefs about beliefs.

Reality leaves a lot to the imagination.

—John Lennon

1

Beliefs Are Models

THE BLIND MEN AND THE ELEPHANT

There is an ancient story called *The Blind Men and the Elephant*. It's told often, so it's likely you have heard it, but it's an important story to understand, so I will repeat it just in case.

A king calls for the blind men of the capital to be brought to his palace. He has an elephant brought in and asks the men to describe it. The king asks the blind men, "Can you tell me, what sort of thing is an elephant?" One man, who felt the elephant's head, says it is like a large pot. Another, who felt the tail, says it is like a rope. Another, who felt the ear, says it is like a hand fan. Another, who felt the side, says it is like a wall. More blind men are called, and they say that it is like a pillar, a pipe, and so on. Each describes a different part of the elephant based on his personal experience. The blind men begin to argue and come to blows, each asserting that he is right and the others are wrong.

What is going on in this story? Each blind man has a grip on one aspect of reality, but none of them holds the whole truth. Each man's picture of the elephant is constrained by the boundaries of his own experience.

Why can't they just talk to each other? If they would only compare notes, they could get a better picture of the whole elephant. It probably wouldn't be perfect, but it would be much, much better.

What is wrong with these men?

The problem is that they cannot separate their experiences from reality. Each man experiences something different. One can feel something that is like a fan, another like a rope, another like a pillar, another like a wall. Imagine you were looking at a wall and someone told you it was a pillar. You would think they were insane.

The parable makes sense because we know the men are blind. None of them can see the whole elephant. But the point of the story is not that blind men cannot see. The point of the story is that we are all blind.

Just as one pair of hands cannot touch everything in the world, one pair of eyes cannot see everything in the world. One mind cannot know everything there is to know. We all can grasp some fragments of reality, but none of us have a grasp on reality as a whole.

This is not the same as saying everything is subjective. We can agree that there is a real world, an objective reality that we all share. At the same time, we must confront the fact that as human beings, the ways we *experience* that reality are inherently unique and subjective.

Einstein once said that it was his religion to believe in the existence of a real world, because he could not prove it.[1]

Let's adopt Einstein's religion and assume that we can agree that there is a valid, objective reality. We must still admit that any understanding we can gain of the world will be limited by our point of view. We all know some things, but nobody can know everything. Reality as a whole is unknowable.

For example, if I say the word *elephant*, I am conjuring an idea into your head. This idea is based on the sum total of your life experiences involving elephants. If you have lived or worked in close proximity to elephants for long periods of time, that idea is probably closer to reality than the idea of someone who has never seen an elephant.

1. Albert Einstein and Rabindranath Tagore, "The Nature of Reality."
    www.mindpodnetwork.com/albert-einstein-rabindranath-tagore-nature-reality/

Having an idea of an elephant in your head is not the same thing as having a real elephant in your head! But we confuse our ideas about reality with the real thing all the time. Often, this is when we start arguing like those foolish blind men.

This is what the story of the blind men and the elephant is all about. We are all blind. Reality is like the elephant. We may be able to grasp pieces of the truth, but the whole truth about reality is unknowable.

Reality is something that is out there. It has a concrete existence, whether you believe it or not. A belief is something you hold in your mind, a kind of map or model of that external reality. But just as maps and models can be wrong, so can beliefs. And just as following the wrong map can get you into dangerous places, a wrong belief can get you into trouble.

When people confuse their beliefs with reality, they get into arguments and conflicts, sometimes even wars.

Have you ever had an argument with someone in your family—your spouse, your child, or your parent—over something you thought was obvious?

Have you ever seen two people read the same news article, only to get into a heated argument about whether it's true, or what it means? This is especially common among people of different political persuasions. These arguments are based on different beliefs. But because people confuse their beliefs with reality, they say the other side is stupid, evil, or crazy. That's a belief, too, and a very dangerous one.

Have you felt the frustration that the person you are arguing with must be obtuse, an idiot, or simply crazy, amazed that they just can't see something that is blatantly evident and glaringly obvious?

You were engaging in *a battle for the obvious.*

Just because something seems obvious to you doesn't necessarily mean it's so. But in the heat of an argument, when your emotions are aroused, this is nearly impossible to see.

Beliefs are not reality. They are not facts. They are constructions. You construct your beliefs, even though for most people this is an unconscious process. By beliefs, I mean *everything you know*.

BELIEFS ARE
CONSTRUCTIONS

This does not mean that your beliefs are wrong, but it does not mean they are right either. In most cases, the question of whether a belief is right or wrong is a kind of distraction. Like the blind men and the elephant, it's often the case that people see the same thing, but they see it *differently*, and the argument over who is right and wrong distracts them from learning or doing anything productive with the situation they find themselves in.

The obvious is not obvious.

Even the obvious. *Especially* the obvious.

All beliefs are approximations, because the whole of reality is unknowable. Any scientist who is worth her salt will tell you this. Beliefs may have some truth to them, but all of us are fallible, and so are our beliefs.

Buddha said his teachings were like a finger pointing at the moon. The finger is helpful if you want to see the moon, but you should not mistake the finger for the moon.

It's the same with beliefs. They are like fingers pointing at the reality, which is the moon. Do not mistake the belief for the reality!

FINGER   MOON

Liminal thinking is learning to see that there are many "obviouses"— and that what is obvious depends on your experiences and your point of view. It also means cultivating the ability to listen and to pay attention to "obviouses" that are different than yours. If one of the blind men had decided to move in a circle around the elephant, and felt what others were feeling, he would have been operating in a liminal way, challenging his own assumptions and beliefs.

The obvious is not obvious.

EXERCISE

Think of a topic on which you have strong beliefs, like a political opinion or religious belief. Now think of someone you know who holds a different belief. Now, try as earnestly as you can to consider their point of view, either by talking to them or honestly researching the topic. Make a list of valid points from both sides of the argument.

Beliefs are models.

Beliefs seem like perfect representations of the world, but, in fact, they are imperfect models for navigating a complex, multidimensional, unknowable reality.

The map is not the territory.

—Alfred Korzybski

2

Beliefs Are Created

Around noon on August 9, 2014, a hot summer day in Ferguson, Missouri, a young black man named Michael Brown was shot and killed by a white police officer named Darren Wilson.

Although there were several witnesses to the shooting, their stories about what happened varied widely.

In the following days and weeks, the mostly black population clashed with the mostly white police force of Ferguson in an escalating series of protests, riots, and police clamp-downs.

This is not a new pattern in the United States. It is a recurring one that has been happening for years. Even as I write this, a similar pattern is unfolding in Baltimore, after a young black man named Freddie Gray died of a broken neck while in police custody.

Every time something like this happens, a battle for the obvious unfolds in the news media, in living rooms, on social media, and elsewhere.

In one narrative, police are the frontline enforcers of a racist society that systemically oppresses black people, where poverty and hopelessness generate legitimate frustration and anger.

In another narrative, racism may be a real problem, but poor people are responsible for their own poverty and for pulling themselves out of it. The police are just doing their job, and unfortunately, sometimes people get hurt. If people didn't break laws and resist arrest, they wouldn't be hurt by the cops.

There are other narratives, too—many of them, too many to go into here.

The competing narratives are so different that they seem like different versions of reality, which is exactly what they are.

You can see similar battles for the obvious in media and politics all over the world, in debates about taxes, guns, religion, immigration, health care, and foreign policy.

We are like the blind men and the elephant, spouting multiple competing and conflicting narratives, which are unfolding everywhere in society, all the time.

What is wrong with us?

I once asked a neuroscientist, "What's the difference between consciousness and dreaming?"

"Very little," he told me. "In fact," he said, "if you look at an MRI, at the actual brain processes that are happening when you are dreaming and when you are awake, they look almost identical. Only a practiced neuroscientist can tell the difference."

What's going on? Are we walking around dreaming?

It's closer to that than you would think.

ARE WE WALKING AROUND DREAMING?

The obvious is not obvious. It is constructed. We work together, as individuals and in groups, to construct the obvious every day. We band together in "obvious clubs" that defend competing versions of reality. When you walk into your obvious club, you will find people reading the same books, watching the same news channels, and talking to the same people, all of which tends to reinforce the same version of reality.

When you feel that your reality is being threatened, you will often fight to protect it.

So if beliefs are constructed, how does that work?

We construct beliefs slowly, layer by layer, over time, using something I call the *pyramid of belief.* It's based (loosely) on the Ladder of Inference, a concept developed by the late Harvard researcher Chris Argyris, a pioneer in human and organizational development.

REALITY
(THE UNKNOWABLE)

Let's just say this baseline stands for reality, which none of us can ever completely understand. This is the ground that the pyramid is built on.

Starting as a baby, you grow, learn, and go through your life, experiencing reality through your senses and perceptions. Like one of those blind men touching the elephant, your experiences are subsets of reality. They are necessarily limited. Even identical twins will have different experiences over the course of their lives. In addition, your experiences will be limited by the nature and capacity of your perceptive system. You will never be able to track animals with your nose, the way a dog can. What the world smells like to a dog is unimaginable, because we just don't have the same sensory abilities. The differences between how people experience the world are more subtle, but they are just as real.

A neuroscientist named Manfred Zimmermann estimates that our capacity for perceiving information is about 11 million bits per second.[1] That's a lot, but it's still a tiny fraction of the amount of information that's potentially available in any situation.

Your experience of reality is limited by the range of your experience. So let's draw your experience as the base of the pyramid, a platform, resting on the unknowable.

EXPERIENCE

REALITY
(THE UNKNOWABLE)

1. M. Zimmerman, *Neurophysiology of Sensory Systems, Fundamentals of Physiology* (Berlin: Springer, 1986), 68–116.

You are also limited by what you pay attention to. In any given moment, the more you focus on one aspect of your experience, the less you will notice everything else. A simple way of saying this is that you can only focus on one thing at a time. For example, if three people are talking at once, you can't possibly follow all aspects of the conversation. There is only so much your mind can grasp at one time.

So your experiences, which are already a subset of all possible experiences, are further limited by the things that you notice, or pay attention to, within those experiences.

What do you pay attention to? In any situation, you will tend to focus your attention on those things that are most likely to meet your needs.

If you're grocery shopping, for example, you will tend to notice the things that are most relevant to you. Even though you might walk through the entire store, it will be impossible for you to notice everything or remember everything you saw. If you're looking for oranges, for example, you will tend to notice things that are small, round, and orange. If you are on a tight budget, however, you will probably pay closer attention to the things that are on sale. Psychologists call this the *priming effect.*

Zimmermann estimates that your conscious attention has a capacity of about 40 bits per second. That's a tiny, tiny fraction of what you can perceive: 40 bits out of a potential 11 million. That's 10,999,960 bits of information that you sense but don't notice, every second.[2]

Think of your attention as a very thin sliver of your overall experience, like a needle on a record player. It's only able to take in a tiny fraction of what you are experiencing in any given moment.

With that in mind, let's draw your attention as a thin line that rests on the platform of your experience, a line that, at least to some degree, you can control and direct.

2. Ibid.

```
                    | ATTENTION
        _____
       |        EXPERIENCE                  |
   ____|_____|____
                    REALITY
                (THE UNKNOWABLE)
```

Based on those things that you notice, you will form theories and make judgments.

For example, you probably have a theory that when you walk into a grocery store you will be able to buy juice. You can probably walk into a store and find juice pretty quickly. This theory is based on your previous experiences shopping in grocery stores.[3]

From your theories, you make judgments. For example, if you see something that looks like a grocery store, and you believe all grocery stores have juice, then you suppose—make a judgment—that you will be able to walk in and buy juice.

Of course, you might be wrong! Perhaps this one grocery store doesn't stock juice, or it is sold out.

These are the third and fourth parts of the Pyramid of Belief: theories and judgments. You will only make theories and judgments about things that you have paid attention to or that you have noticed.

So let's draw theories and judgments as two more platforms that rest on that needle of attention.

---

3. By the way, most grocery stores put the juice and other commonly purchased items at the back of the store. They do this so you will be forced to walk by a bunch of other things before you get your juice and then walk out, increasing the chances that you will buy something else, too. For more on the science behind store layouts, see *Why We Buy: The Science of Shopping*, by Paco Underhill.

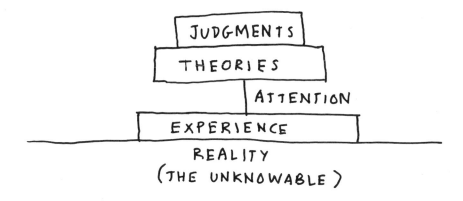

Your experience can be extended, of course, by things teachers tell you, things that you read or see on TV, things that your friends say, what your doctor says, and so on. But each of those sources is also making judgments, based on their own Belief Pyramids. So you will also need to make theories and judgments about which sources you trust and which you don't.

Even if you trust your doctor, for example, you may still want to get a second opinion on issues that are very important to you.

These four things—your experiences, attention, theories, and judgments—form a foundation that reduces the unknowable to a kind of map or model that is simple enough to understand and use in daily life.

In essence, as people, we simplify reality to reduce its infinite complexity, in order to make it easier to understand.

This is important, and there's nothing wrong with it. In fact, it's essential. We all need this simplified reality in order to function. If you experienced everything as if it were completely new, you would be like a baby, helpless, paralyzed by complexity, and unable to do anything.

But it's also important to realize that this Pyramid of Belief reduces reality from infinite complexity to a small set of theories, which form the foundations on which you (and everyone else) construct our beliefs.

So let's draw one more platform to represent the set of beliefs you hold at any one point in time.

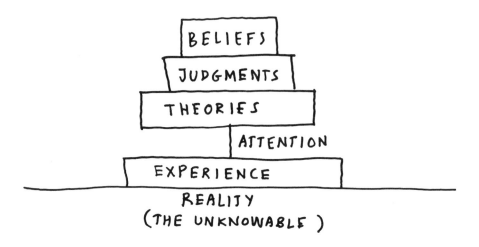

As I said earlier, it's easy to confuse your beliefs with reality, and that's what most people do.

This situation happens because the people in your social circle tend to have had similar experiences, and one of the ways we reinforce beliefs is by sharing experiences and talking to each other about what they mean.

Your beliefs form the fundamental model that you use to navigate the world, to think about things, to decide what to do and what to avoid, like a map. We form a lot of these beliefs by middle childhood.[4]

And since you're the one who built the map, it's natural to believe that it corresponds to the territory that you are navigating. After all, most of the time, your map gets you where you want to go. So much so that when the map doesn't get you where you want to go, the first thing you question is not the map but reality.

4. John H. Flavell, "Cognitive Development: Children's Knowledge About the Mind," *Annual Review of Psychology*, Vol. 50 (February 1999): 21–45.

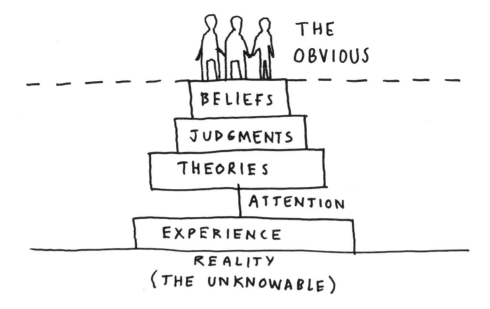

Here's a picture of you and me, or anyone at all really, because this is all of us, standing on top of our self-constructed Pyramid of Belief, living in the land of the obvious.

We feel that we're standing on solid ground here. We think that the ground is reality, that it's obvious. But we actually constructed this reality. Your "obvious" is one of many versions, and other people have different ones.

The space between the baseline of reality and "the obvious" is liminal space. These needs, feelings, and thoughts happen inside you. If you don't talk about them, they are invisible to others.

Learning how to navigate this "below the obvious" construction zone is one of the core skills of liminal thinking.

Liminal thinking requires you to become more conscious of that invisible belief construction process, in yourself and others.

EXERCISE

Take a belief that you hold and try to deconstruct it. What personal experiences created that belief? What did you notice in those experiences? What theories and judgments have you made that support that belief? Can you imagine other kinds of experiences which might have led to different constructions?

Beliefs are created.

Beliefs are constructed hierarchically, using theories and judgments, which are based on selected facts and personal, subjective experiences.

Our beliefs guide our desires
and shape our actions.

—Charles S. Peirce

3

Beliefs Create a Shared World

A belief is a story in your head. Even dogs have beliefs. I'll give you an example. About a year ago, we adopted a 6-year-old dog. He was a rescue dog. Rescue dogs come with a history, from their life before, and you don't always know what happened to them in the past. The dog's name was Spitfire. Spitfire seemed like a great dog.

It was New Year's Eve. We had a special dinner for all of our family, and my wife thought, let's do something special for the dog. She got a big bone, a New Year's bone, for the dog. What do you expect is going to happen when you give a dog a bone? He'll chew it. He'll get excited, right? He's going to be happy.

What happened? We gave this dog that big bone, and he just turned evil. He grabbed the bone. He growled. He ran off with the bone and started chewing it in a corner of the room. My son walked up to him to reassure him, saying, "Hey, Spitfire, it's okay." The dog snarled, and jumped up and bit him. He attacked him. He thought my son was trying to take his bone away.

This dog had a belief, a story, in his head. The story in his head probably was something like, if I get something good, I better protect it. And anyone who tries to approach me is probably trying to take it away.

Obviously, the dog was reacting in a way that was inappropriate for the situation, right? Protecting his bone was probably a good strategy in his past situation. But in this situation, it was not the right thing to do. The old threat was no longer there. But the dog did not know that.

A belief is a story in your head, a cause-and-effect chain, like a recipe or rule for action.

The basic recipe looks like this: If you have a need, then look for a belief that provides a rule for action to get the result that you want.

Many beliefs take the form of "If x, then y." A very simple example would be, if you are hungry (need), then eat (belief). If you follow the implicit rule and eat (action) and that causes you to feel less hungry (result), your belief has been validated.

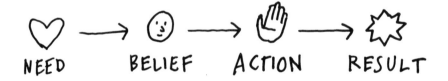

Where do needs come from? They come from your experience of the world. They come from your feelings. You feel hungry, or tired, or lonely, or anxious, or a million other things.

The most acute and persistent needs are the ones you pay attention to. Let's go with hunger because it's a super-simple example. When you're hungry, you will tend to pay more attention to things in your environment that are food-related. Say, a restaurant, or grocery store, or the cupboard in the kitchen.

Let's say you are out and about, and you're hungry but short on cash. You're going to rely on your past experiences and beliefs about the kinds of places where you can quickly get some food for the lowest price.

When you put those beliefs into action, you are going to create some kinds of results in the world. If you are able to satisfy your hunger without spending too much, you've got a strategy that works. That's an effective belief—one that works.

If you go to a fast food place, and it satisfies your hunger, but the food also makes you sick, then you learned something there, too. I'll bet you're not going back to that place next time you're hungry.

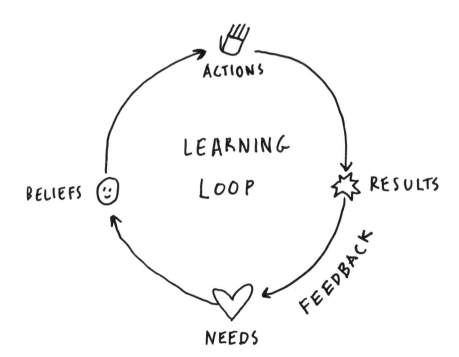

This is the basic way that we learn how to be effective in life. It's called a *learning loop*: a continuous feedback cycle of needs, thinking, and action. It's the way we learn how to act, to give us the best chance to get what we want out of any situation.

Over time, that learning loop feedback cycle creates habits of belief and behavior.

Now I'd like to connect this idea of the learning loop with the pyramid of belief, because they are connected concepts.

Learning loops start when you feel a need. That happens at the base of the pyramid. You have experiences, and you pay attention to the things most likely to meet your needs.

Those needs become beliefs through the process of exploring theories and making judgments. Then, as you act on those beliefs and experience the results, you interpret what happened as part of your learning process.

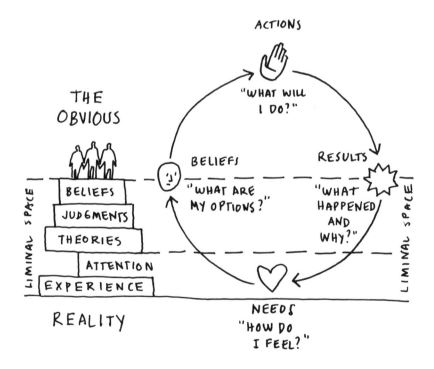

Beliefs cause behavior. That's the point of the dog story. Without knowing the dog's history, you just see the behavior, and you have to guess where that behavior is coming from. You don't know the history, so you have no context for understanding the belief.

My first thought in Spitfire's case was this: we need to get rid of this dog. It's a problem dog. I almost took him back to the pound. That's a belief too, right? "Spitfire is a problem dog" is a belief. If I had acted on that belief, it could have started a chain reaction that made it come true.

Let's say my belief was "Spitfire is a problem dog," and that the way to fix that problem was by punishing him, say by taking the bone away.

In that case, my reaction would probably reinforce Spitfire's existing belief: that he needed to protect the bone. So he would continue the bad behavior. In fact, it would probably get worse. The more his bone was taken away, the more he would feel the need to protect it.

In that case, his behavior would reinforce my belief that he's a problem dog, and so on. This is where learning loops go wrong, creating a vicious cycle called a *doom loop*.

When two or more learning loops interact like this, they form a system of belief and behavior that I call a *story web*: a shared world that is co-created by the people (or dogs) who participate in it. This shared world can seem as if it is just "the way it is," when in fact it is just one of many possible realities.

Happily, the dog story turned out differently. We found this local guy—some people called him the *dog whisperer*—and had him come out to our house. He explained how the dog had probably come from a difficult circumstance, and he told me that we could have a great relationship with this dog, but we needed to invest in the dog the same way we would invest in any other relationship: quality time.

"If you spend 20 minutes a day with this dog," he said, "working with him, training him, you will see him change dramatically."

"He needs quality time" is a different belief. It starts from a different premise. It's not "Spitfire is a problem dog" so much as "He's a smart dog, who, with a little help, is capable of learning new behaviors."

Well, that's the belief we acted on. Every day my wife and I spent time with the dog, training him, teaching him how to behave, and rewarding good behavior with treats. Turns out he was a very smart dog, and he learned quickly.

One of Spitfire's doom loops had to do with other dogs. He pretty much saw other dogs as a threat, probably because somewhere in his history other dogs meant competition for scraps of food.

So when I would take him for a walk, I started carrying treats along with me. Whenever we saw another dog, I would give them both treats. Slowly, over time, Spitfire rewired his brain from "another dog is a threat" to "another dog is a good thing." By reinforcing this positive behavior, we were able to turn that doom loop around. Now it's a *delight loop*: a self-reinforcing pattern of positive belief and behavior. Nowadays, whenever Spitfire sees another dog, he is super-excited and looks forward to making a new friend.

He still has trouble once in a while, like anyone who has had a traumatic history, but that dog has truly transformed. He is a different dog because he has changed his beliefs to better match up with the environment he is living in these days.

This is what I mean when I say a story web is one possible version of reality. There were at least two possible worlds I could have created here, one called "problem dog," and another called "good dog." One belief leads to a doom loop, the other to a delight loop.

TWO POSSIBLE WORLDS

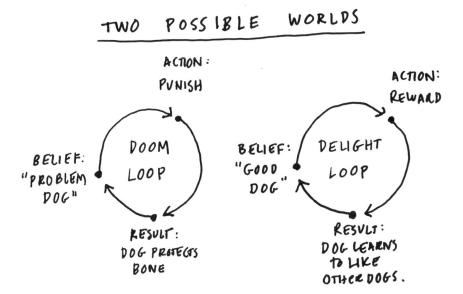

Based on the belief I chose, I could have created either one of those worlds.

If I had chosen to believe Spitfire was a problem dog and I had acted on that belief, it would have been a self-fulfilling prophecy. By my belief and actions, I would have created that world. But I chose to believe Spitfire was a good dog, and acted accordingly. By those actions, my wife and I created that more positive shared world, with a lot of help from the dog, of course.

That is the power of a story web. Changing stories can change reality.

We co-create shared worlds like this all the time. Usually, you don't notice them. They are so embedded in routines that they become invisible. They are social agreements that normally go unspoken. When you walk into a Starbucks, for example, you know what to do: where to stand, how to order, whether to tip, where to wait, and so on.

Have you ever walked into a coffee shop, or a restaurant, and you couldn't figure out where the line was? This happens once in a while, right? It happens to me a lot when I travel. I walk into a place, and I'm not sure if it's a sit-down restaurant where someone will come to take your order, or if it's the kind of place where you order at the counter, or maybe something else. It's not always clear, especially when the signs are in a language you don't understand.

This happens when you don't understand the rules of that shared world.

Most human relationships are a lot more complex than the relationship you have with a dog. You have a lot less control over the situation, for one thing. And you can't just walk around with cookies in your pocket, changing people's behavior by giving them treats (although I doubt it would hurt!).

But the same principles apply: Your beliefs inform your actions, and your actions are interpreted by others, and those interpretations become the basis for their beliefs, which inform their actions. Here's an example we're all familiar with. A child throws a tantrum in the grocery store.

The kid wants candy or whatever. She sees something, and she wants it. So the story in the kid's head is, "I want this thing and I'm going to assert myself. I'm going to create a scene," and different parents have different ways of reacting, right?

What's the parent's story? "Everyone's looking at me. This is really embarrassing. I can have a fight, right here, right now, or I can give in. I've had a long day, and I'm not in the mood for this. I can give the kid what he wants and fight this battle another time."

Sometimes you do, sometimes you don't, but whatever you do, you're creating a story web. If you give in to the kid's demands, you are reinforcing a learning loop that will probably come back to haunt you later.

The parent has a story that's something like, "Okay, just this once. Just this once."

The kid has a story that says, "I can just escalate this until I get what I want. I can yell louder, and if necessary, I can throw myself on the ground and scream until I get what I want."

Even though neither the kid nor the parent really wants a tantrum, even though that's not the goal for anyone, together they are co-creating a tantrum-creation system. Any human group that spends enough time together, whether it's a family, a team, or a company, will inevitably co-create these kinds of story webs.

This is the way story webs create a shared world. Learning loops can reinforce good habits and bad habits alike. They are co-created by the people (and dogs!) who participate in them. They are a by-product of ongoing interactions.

Over time, these beliefs and actions become deeply embedded habits and routines: a complex, dense, interconnected system of beliefs and behavior that is not easy to untangle and understand. The more we reinforce those habits and routines, the more invisible they become, until one day they are just "the way it is." But to practice liminal thinking, it's important to remember that "the way it is" is something that we have created together, and if we can create it, we can change it.

EXERCISE

Think of a doom loop that repeats itself somewhere in your life, with a friend, family member, or co-worker. Sketch a diagram of the doom loop pattern. Then try to draw another diagram that turns that doom loop into a delight loop. What alternative shared worlds can you imagine? What could you do differently to escape the doom loop?

Beliefs create a shared world.

Beliefs are the psychological material we use to co-create a shared world, so we can live, work, and do things together. Changing a shared world requires changing its underlying beliefs.

The question is not what you look at, but what you see.

—Henry David Thoreau

4

Beliefs Create
Blind Spots

In the early 1990s, I worked as a news artist at a newspaper called the *Seattle Post-Intelligencer*. Even then, it was clear that the newspaper industry was in trouble, so I decided that it was time I found a different career. One of the careers I was thinking about was becoming a university professor. I went to the local university and found an art teacher so I could learn more about it.

He wasn't very encouraging. He showed me a big stack of resumes and told me, in a very condescending way, that his department received hundreds of applications for every open position, that these positions opened very rarely, and anyway, he didn't think I was qualified.

Then I spoke with a friend who was teaching art at a local college. He told me there was no way I would be able to get a job as a university teacher without a master's degree (which I didn't have).

I didn't think he was wrong, but I decided to test his belief.

Here's why: I thought, it's a lot quicker and easier to apply for a job than it is to get a master's degree. I know how to apply for a job, so I'll just try that and see what happens. If it turns out my friend is right, then I haven't really lost anything. I still can go get a master's degree. But if he's wrong, I will have saved myself a lot of time and money.

Can you guess the ending? Yes, I got a teaching job without having a master's degree.

My friend wasn't lying to me or trying to mislead me. He was trying to help, by sharing his knowledge about the situation, which was greater than mine. But that knowledge also included a set of beliefs about what was possible, or, perhaps I should say, *impossible*. His beliefs created a constraint that made certain actions—like applying for a teaching job without a master's degree—inconceivable, or absurd.

My friend had a limiting belief—a belief that narrowed the range of possibilities.

Let's say I had taken my friend's word for it that I needed a master's degree. That would have created a boundary around what I was able to conceive as possible. That boundary would have reduced the scope and range of my thinking. If I had accepted that limiting belief, I might have spent at least two years and who knows how much money on something that was unnecessary. Or maybe I would not have applied for a teaching job at all, because I would have seen a master's degree as an expensive, futile effort that made no sense.

A LIMITING BELIEF

Beliefs are necessary. We couldn't survive without them. They are tools for thinking. We use them to navigate the world, and they guide our actions. But they also limit us. In fact, the words *liminal* and *limit* are linked; they share the same Latin root. The same boundaries that make it possible for us to think also limit what we can conceive.

Even your closest friends, with the best of intentions, may have limiting beliefs that close off possibilities and opportunities that would otherwise be open to you.

This is what I mean by thresholds and doorways. There are opportunities around you all the time, every day, and in many cases you are unable to see them, because limiting beliefs blind you to real possibilities.

Liminal thinking is a way to identify limiting beliefs and open yourself to hitherto unseen possibilities that can open new doors.

EXERCISE

Think about the people in your life, friends, family, and co-workers. Do the people in your life have beliefs that might be limiting you? Make a list of those beliefs. Can you think of alternative beliefs that might also be valid? What about your own beliefs? Do you have beliefs that might be constraining or limiting your potential, or the potential of others you care about?

Beliefs create blind spots.

Beliefs are tools for thinking and provide rules for action, but they can also create artificial constraints that blind you to valid possibilities.

Reality is that which,
when you stop believing in it,
doesn't go away.

—Philip K. Dick

5

Beliefs Defend Themselves

B etween 2003 and 2005, researchers conducted a series of studies comparing how Democrats and Republicans interpreted facts about the war in Iraq.[1] The researchers were interested in what happens when people encounter new information, especially when it contradicts their existing beliefs.

The original invasion was justified in no small part by the Bush administration's claim that Iraq was concealing weapons of mass destruction (WMDs) and posed a threat to the United States.

The U.S. did not find any WMDs, and as the war continued, it seemed increasingly unlikely that WMDs would be found.

1. "Same Facts, Different Interpretations: Partisan Motivation and Opinion on Iraq," http://dx.doi.org/10.1111/j.1468-2508.2007.00601.x.

Neither Republicans nor Democrats challenged these facts. But they had very different interpretations. Democrats concluded that the WMDs had not existed. Republicans concluded that Iraq had moved the WMDs, or destroyed them, or that they had not yet been found. When it became increasingly clear over time that no WMDs would be found, Republican explanations shifted to "Well, there must have been a reason or we wouldn't have gone in!"

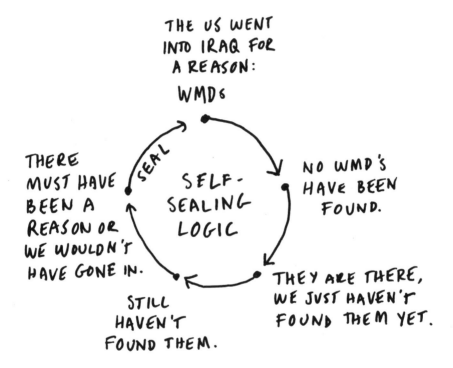

This isn't just a Republican phenomenon. For the purposes of comparison, the researchers looked at Democrat and Republican attitudes during the 1995 Clinton-led U.S. intervention in the Bosnian conflict and found similar dynamics. They wrote:

"In short, Democrats and Republicans flip when attention shifts from Bosnia to Iraq, as the president responsible for the intervention changes from a Democrat to a Republican. Citizens set aside general partisan values about war and intervention—if any such values exist—to support their party's position in each conflict."[2]

Whatever groups you belong to or most strongly associate with, the dynamics will be similar. Collectively, we create a kind of *bubble of belief* that reinforces and protects our existing beliefs by denying that alternative beliefs are within the realm of possibility. It's a kind of collective delusion or dream that we co-create in order to maintain a group map that we use to navigate the world.

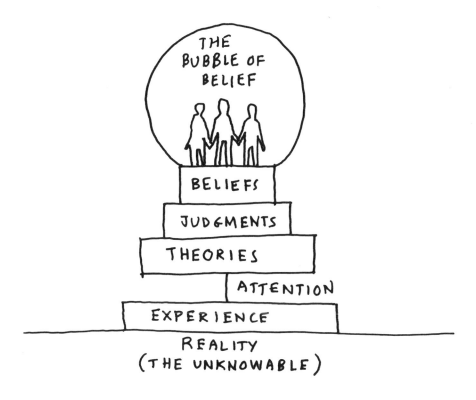

It's a bit like living in a snow globe. If you shake it up, you will get a lot of noise in there as people try to convince themselves that their beliefs are an accurate depiction of reality.

2. Ibid.

Argyris called this *self-sealing logic*, or, when applied to organizations, *organizational defensive routines*.[3]

In order to maintain a sense of certainty and control, as well as a collective self-image of who we are and what we stand for, we work together to create and maintain this shared map of reality. You probably have more than one shared map that you use to navigate different areas in your life—one that you share with your family, one you share with friends, another one you share with co-workers.

These shared maps are useful because they allow us to do things together, based on shared assumptions. They are also efficient, because they save us from asking questions all the time, so we can get on with our work.

But a shared map also has some dangers, especially when, over time, the map begins to get out of sync with what's really going on. And the longer a group of people have been operating with a shared map, the more likely there will be a mismatch between the map and reality.

People like stability. Once a group of people has formed a belief, they will tend to reinforce it in a way that creates blind spots to alternative beliefs.

In his book, *The Future of Management*, Gary Hamel tells the story of a conversation he had with senior auto executives in Detroit.[4] He asked them why, after 20 years of benchmarking studies, their company had been unable to catch up to Toyota's productivity. Here's what they said:

> Twenty years ago, we started sending our young people to Japan to study Toyota. They'd come back and tell us how good Toyota was, and we simply didn't believe them. We figured they'd dropped a zero somewhere—no one could produce cars with so few defects per vehicle, or with so few labor hours.

3. Chris Argyris, *Organizational Traps: Leadership, Culture, Organizational Design*, 1st ed. (Oxford, UK: Oxford University Press, 2012).
4. Gary Hamel, *The Future of Management*, 1st ed. (Brighton, MA: Harvard Business Review Press, 2007).

It was five years before we acknowledged that Toyota really was beating us in a bunch of critical areas. Over the next five years, we told ourselves that Toyota's advantages were all cultural. It was all about *wa* and *nemawashi*—the uniquely Japanese spirit of cooperation and consultation that Toyota had cultivated with its employees. We were sure that American workers would never put up with these paternalistic practices.

Then, of course, Toyota started building plants in the United States, and they got the same results here they got in Japan—so our cultural excuse went out the window. For the next five years, we focused on Toyota's manufacturing processes. We studied their use of factory automation, their supplier relationships, just-in-time systems, everything. But despite all our benchmarking, we could never seem to get the same results in our own factories.

It's only in the last five years that we've finally admitted to ourselves that Toyota's success is based on a wholly different set of principles—about the capabilities of its employees and the responsibilities of its leaders.

I had a similar experience. I was working on a project at Nokia when the iPhone was first announced. I asked a senior executive in the company, "Aren't you worried about Apple getting into the phone business?"

He said, "No, we're not worried. They are just going to increase the market for smart phones, and ours is better."

The company at the time had 40 percent share of the global smart phone market. Today they have less than one percent.

This is self-sealing logic at work. New information from outside the bubble of belief is discounted, or distorted, because it conflicts with the version of reality that exists inside the bubble.

This has to do with the way people evaluate new information. There are two ways that people make sense of new ideas:

- **First, is it internally coherent?** Does it make sense, given what I already know, and can it be integrated with all of my other beliefs? In other words, does it make sense from within my bubble?

- **Second, is it externally valid?** Can I test it? If I try it, does it work? This is an excellent way to test a new idea, but one big problem, which causes blind spots and reinforces those self-sealing bubbles, is that people rarely test ideas for external validity when they don't have internal coherence.

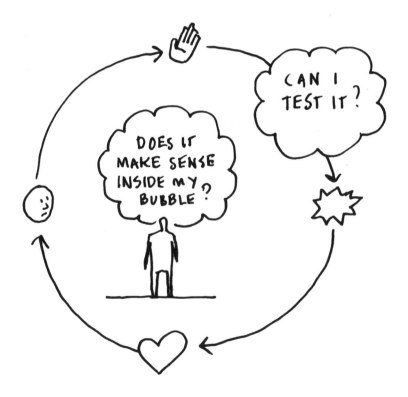

That concept is important enough that I'm going to say it again:

> *People rarely test ideas for external validity when they don't*
> *have internal coherence.*

If it doesn't make sense from within the bubble, you're going to think it's a mistake, or a lie, or somebody got it wrong. You will tend to do whatever is necessary to protect the consistency and coherence of that bubble, because to you, *that bubble is reality itself.*

Liminal thinking requires a willingness to test and validate new ideas, even when they seem absurd, crazy, or wrong.

EXERCISE

Think about your relationships with friends, family, and co-workers. What beliefs do you share? When those beliefs are questioned, how are they defended? Think of a core belief and sketch a diagram of the self-sealing logic that is typically used to defend it.

Beliefs defend themselves.

Beliefs are unconsciously defended by a bubble of self-sealing logic, which maintains them even when they are invalid, to protect personal identity and self-worth.

If you want to change the world, change yourself.

—Tom Robbins

6

Beliefs Are Tied to Identity

The car service Uber recently started doing business in my hometown of St. Louis. I decided to give it a try.

The driver who picked me up was an older guy named John. He was driving a Ford Taurus. I suspect he was retired. I got in the front seat. As he drove me to my destination, we started talking about St. Louis. Many of the places we drove by had recently gone out of business or changed hands from one business to another. John knew a lot about each business, who had owned it, what happened to it, when it was sold, and so on.

As he told me the stories of the various businesses we passed, I learned that he had tried some entrepreneurial things—like starting a business and investing in other people's schemes—that had not worked out so well for him.

Gradually, the conversation began to move from small talk to what I can only call conspiracy theories. The Federal Reserve. Monetary policy. Several times, he said, "Most people don't understand what's really going on."

I asked him to explain, and as he did, it became more and more clear to me that his theories were muddled and confused. I couldn't understand how they made sense, even to him. But they did. To him, they seemed clear.

They boiled down to "Everything is going to hell." He seemed certain that some kind of societal collapse was imminent.

We drove by some mansions, and he said, shaking his head, "A few years ago you could buy one of these for almost nothing." Trying to suspend my disbelief and going with his theory, I said, "Well, maybe soon, when everything collapses, they will be cheap again, right?"

Although this would seem to fit his theory, he shook his head. It didn't seem like he wanted to hear that.

The conversation ended when we reached my destination, and he awkwardly made some kind of comment about the Uber review system. I think he was worried that I would give him a bad rating. (I didn't, I gave him five stars for being interesting.)

His theories seemed muddled and fuzzy to me. But they were deeply meaningful, to him.

What was John's core belief? I don't know for sure, but here's one theory: I don't think John is happy with his situation in life. And like most people, he wants to believe that he is important, that he matters. If his sense of importance is based on his success in business, which, so far, has eluded him, then that's a feeling that threatens his sense of self-worth.

So at a deeply personal level, John needs a belief that affirms that he matters, and that also explains why he has not had the kinds of successes he wanted in life.

Beliefs are explanations of the world. When an emotional need is unfulfilled—especially when it remains unfulfilled for some time—the brain seeks to fill that gap with some kind of explanation.

Numerous studies have found that when people feel a lack of control, they have an increased propensity to form conspiracy theories as a way to explain their helplessness.[1, 2, 3]

Think about it: When you are doing everything you can to fulfill an unmet need, and you are not having success or feeling any traction, you look for reasons. Something must be blocking you. What could it be?

The conspiracy theory arises to fill that gap. It explains why you are not getting what you want. Conspiracy theories thrive within groups who feel that they don't have control over their lives. A belief that is deeply tied to identity and feelings of self-worth is called a *governing belief*.

Superficial, surface beliefs are relatively easy to change. You don't have so much invested in them. But some beliefs are deeply connected with your sense of self, your identity. They define who you are. Those are the beliefs that are most deep-rooted and hard to change, because to change them would mean changing how you see yourself.

The deeper you go in exploring anyone's belief system (including your own!), the closer you will get to their governing beliefs. The more foundational the belief, the more it will be unconsciously defended by self-sealing logic. This can be a scary place to go.

1. Jennifer A. Whitson and Adam D. Galinsky, "Lacking Control Increases Illusory Pattern Perception," *Science*, Vol. 322 (October 2008): 115–117.
2. Daniel Sullivan, Mark J. Landau, and Zachary K. Rothschild, "An Existential Function of Enemyship: Evidence That People Attribute Influence to Personal and Political Enemies to Compensate for Threats to Control," *Journal of Personality and Social Psychology*, Vol. 98 (March 2010): 434–439.
3. Aaron E. Kay, et al., "Compensatory Control: Achieving Order Through the Mind, Our Institutions, and the Heavens," *Current Directions in Psychological Science*, Vol 18 (October 2009): 264–268.

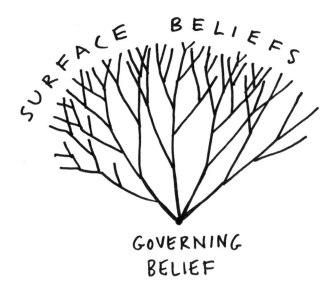

GOVERNING
BELIEF

Questioning your governing beliefs can lead to profound change, but because so many other beliefs are based on them, there's a lot at stake—and not just for yourself.

Your governing beliefs are part of the story webs that hold your relationships together. They connect you to your family, your friends, your co-workers, and your community. Challenging a governing belief can threaten the stability of those relationships and the shared world that keeps them functioning. It has the potential to bring your whole world crashing down.

In fact, governing beliefs are so important to group cohesion that their very existence depends on *not talking about them.* The governing beliefs usually sit comfortably out of sight, and are never discussed. When someone brings them up, they can be faced with rage, sometimes violence, and expulsion from the group.

Here's a very simple, classic example. The CEO says "everyone's equal here," but the CEO has perks that others don't, like the corner office, private parking space, and so on. Everyone knows this, but nobody brings it up.

In the early 1950s, a woman named Dorothy Martin began to receive spirit messages from spiritual beings of superior intelligence and wisdom, called the Guardians of Earth, who communicated to her through a kind of automatic writing. The Guardians told her that they were beings of light, and that the world, which had become corrupted, would be destroyed in a cataclysmic flood on December 21, 1954. The Guardians promised her, though, that they would come down in flying saucers to rescue her and her followers before the floodwaters subsumed the Earth.

On December 20, Dorothy received a series of messages from the Guardians. The Seekers should remove all metal from their persons. A spaceman would knock on the door of her house at midnight and escort the Seekers to a flying saucer, which would be parked nearby. That evening the group gathered together at Dorothy's house. At 11:15 Dorothy received a message that everyone should get their coats and stand by.

Midnight passed. No spaceman knocked on the door. The Seekers continued to wait. At 4 a.m., Dorothy broke down into tears. She told her followers that she knew some were beginning to doubt, but that they must beam light on those who needed it most and hold the group together.

At 4:45 Dorothy received a message from the Guardians. The message said that the group had beamed so much light and goodness into the world during their late-night vigil that they had saved the world from destruction. The members of the group, who had previously shunned inquiries from the press, were overwhelmed with a sense of urgency to tell the story of salvation to the people of Earth.

By 6:30 a.m. they had called all of the local newspapers as well as the national wire services to share the good news.[4]

4. Leon Festinger, Henry Reicken, and Stanley Schachter, *When Prophecy Fails* (New York: Harper & Row, 1956).

Governing beliefs form the foundation of your (version of) reality. They generate feelings of self-worth, group identity, and social stability. They give order and meaning to life. When you feel that your governing beliefs are threatened, it's like you, yourself, are being threatened.

The deeper you go, the scarier it gets, but at the same time, the greater the potential for change. It's not intuitive, but Liminal Thinking requires courage: When your beliefs are being threatened, and your instinct says "defend the belief," you need to go toward that fear if you want to open the door to lasting change.

A truly significant change to your world will almost always require some kind of corresponding change to your self.

EXERCISE

Make a list of what you think your governing beliefs are. What are your core beliefs? What beliefs make you the person that you are and create the foundations for your choices in life, large and small? Then sit down with a friend, someone you trust. Tell them what a governing belief is and ask them what they think yours are. Compare their observations with yours.

Beliefs are tied to identity.

Governing beliefs, which form the basis for other beliefs, are the most difficult to change, because they are tied to personal identity and feelings of self-worth. You can't change your governing beliefs without changing yourself.

2

What to Do About It

These nine practices will help you minimize reality distortion, envision possibilities, and create positive change.

Lying to ourselves is more deeply ingrained than lying to others.

—Fyodor Dostoyevsky

1

Assume That You Are Not Objective

Culture change expert Carolyn Taylor told me this story about a senior executive who didn't like bad news. When he heard bad news, he had a tendency to shoot the messenger. Over time, people started keeping bad news to themselves. They would sugarcoat their messages or conceal information that might upset the boss. When he came to Carolyn for help, can you guess how he described the problem?

Here's what he said: "I don't feel like I know what's going on in my organization. People are not keeping me in the loop, and they are hiding information from me."

He didn't realize—at least, not at first—that his behavior was causing the very problem he wanted to solve. He had a very big blind spot.

THE JOHARI WINDOW

	KNOWN BY YOU	UNKNOWN BY YOU
KNOWN TO OTHERS	**OPEN** KNOWN BY BOTH YOU AND OTHERS	**BLIND SPOT** UNKNOWN TO YOU BUT KNOWN BY OTHERS
UNKNOWN TO OTHERS	**HIDDEN** KNOWN TO YOU BUT NOT BY OTHERS	**UNKNOWN** UNKNOWN BY BOTH YOU AND OTHERS

The Johari window is a framework developed by two psychologists named Joe and Harry (really!)[1] as an aid for understanding the self. It's a great tool for liminal thinking. You can imagine it as a building with four rooms.

One room is open. This represents things that both you and others know about you. For example, this might include your job title, your hair color, and so on. You might say this is the "public" you.

Another room is hidden. This represents things you know about yourself that others don't know. This might include feelings that you don't share, or other things you conceal from others. This is the "private" you.

---

1. J. Luft and H. Ingham, "The Johari Window, A Graphic Model of Interpersonal Awareness," Proceeedings of the Western Laboratory in Group Development, UCLA, Los Angeles, CA, 1955.

Another room is unknown. This represents the things that you don't know about yourself, and neither does anyone else. You may have feelings that you are not aware of, or you may be capable of things that you don't know you are capable of. This is the "unknown" you.

The last room is your blind spot. This represents the things that others can see about you, but that you are unaware of. Maybe people see you as pushy but don't tell you. This is the public self that you are unaware of.

These blind spots can be crippling to your effectiveness. Blind spots cut both ways, of course. People can have blinds spots about you—things they can't see about you, for example, due to their own beliefs.

It's very easy to see problems and logical inconsistencies in other people. It's very hard to see them in yourself.

This illusion of objectivity is often particularly acute in senior leaders, because there's a tendency for people to tell them what they want to hear.

Many problems that senior leaders most want to solve are, at least partially, and usually unconsciously, caused by their own behavior. So if you have a persistent problem that keeps popping up and seems intractable, start by assuming that you are not objective.

Think about it. If you care enough to try to solve a problem, then it matters to you. If it matters to you, it must affect you in some way. If it affects you strongly, that means that you are probably not outside the problem. You are inside of it. You're a part of it, probably in ways you are not fully aware of.

So often, we try to solve problems as if we are outside them. When people describe a problem, you will often see them pointing away from themselves. You will hear the word *them* a lot. That's because "they" are seen as the problem. But in most cases, "they" are only one part of the problem. The problems that are most resistant to solutions are system problems. In a system problem, if you're part of the system, you're part of the problem.

Your biggest blind spot is yourself.

If you are not willing to look at your own contributions and inputs to the situation as part of the problem, you won't be able to see it clearly. Your understanding will be distorted and so will your beliefs.

EXERCISE

Make copies of the "character traits" list in the appendix and give the list to a few close friends that you trust. Go down the list and check all the traits that you think apply to you. Have your friends do the same (traits that apply to you, not them). Then compare the lists. Traits that show up on your list but not any of theirs are *hidden*. Traits that show up on both yours and theirs are *open*. Traits that show up on their lists but not yours are *blind spots*. Traits that show up on none of the lists are potential *unknowns*. Make a large drawing of the Johari window and fill in the traits. What insights does it give you?

Assume that you are not objective.

If you're part of the system you want to change, you're part of the problem.

A genuine relationship is one that is not dominated by the ego with its image-making and self-seeking. In a genuine relationship, there is an outward flow of open, alert attention toward the other person in which there is no wanting whatsoever.

—Eckhart Tolle

2

Empty Your Cup

Erica Kochi leads Unicef's innovation team.

In the early 2000s, she led a project called *Our Stories*.
The goal was to collect stories from the people of Uganda
and share them with the rest of the world. They had the
support of Google, and free laptops were being provided by
a non-profit called One Laptop per Child. The team went
out to farmers and people in rural areas to give people these
laptops so they could record their stories.

What do you think happened? First, the laptops had a terrible user interface, and they were hard to use. So nobody used them. The people said, "I don't want to tell my story. Why should I tell my story to a bunch of foreigners?" They didn't see how telling their story was going to help them in their daily lives. They said, "What I want is someone to come out and fix these potholes. I want clean water. Street lights."

The project was a failure, as a project. But as a learning experience, it was invaluable.

The next time Unicef did something in Uganda, they made sure they understood the situation. Instead of bringing in new technology like laptops, they built their program on technology people already knew and used in Uganda, such as mobile phones and text messages. It's easy for people to join: They simply text JOIN to an SMS short code, and once a week they get a question by text message, which can be anything from "Do you have access to fresh water?" to "Are there medicines and drugs at the nearby clinic?" to "What's your view on corporal punishment?"

The entire Ugandan government is in the system, so they have a real-time picture of the state of the nation and people's attitudes about health conditions, education, government services, and so on. The results of the weekly surveys are published in the newspapers and on TV. They even had new bills introduced into Parliament because of information gathered through this program.

There's real feedback and people are involved because the program was designed based on a real understanding of the situation rather than just good intentions.

The most common mistake I see people make in change efforts is to assume that they understand the situation. Sometimes they see a problem one way, when the problem is seen very differently by others. Sometimes other people don't see a problem at all, or they see a different problem.

For example, in Erica's case, her team went in with an initial assumption, a belief, that the people of Uganda would want to tell their stories. That wasn't so. But once Unicef had gotten past their assumptions and started to listen, they were able to understand a different problem.

I have a friend named Mick Calder. He works at a company called the 333 Group, in Melbourne, Australia. Mick is a turnaround guy. If you're running a company, Mick is the last guy you want to meet, because if you meet him, it means you're probably in trouble. You meet Mick when you have run out of other options.

Once you meet Mick, his organization will offer you two alternatives. The first is that they can take you into bankruptcy. They will help you liquidate the company; help you through the legal and financial aspects of that choice. The second option is that they will take the company away from you and turn it around. What this means is that they will buy you out of debt, and in exchange for taking on your debt, they will own the company.

Mick's company is very good at this. They have turned a lot of companies around. I was very curious about this.

I asked Mick: "When you take over a company, you know nothing about it, while the people you are taking it over from have been there for many years—sometimes as long as 40 or 50 years. And yet you are able to turn it around, while they, with all of their knowledge and experience, were not able to do so. How is it possible that you can succeed where they have failed?"

I also asked him, "What do you do differently? How are you able to come in and make positive change happen so quickly?"

Mick told me that by the time his team arrives in a company, the people who work there are ready for change. Mick and his people go in and they listen. They talk to employees. They talk to customers. And, he told me, customers and employees, between them, always know what needs to be done.

You listen? I asked. So simple? How can that be?

Mick told me that it's very rare for the team that got the company into trouble to be able to turn it around. Chances are that they were successful before they started having problems. Sometime in the past, they had hit on something that worked well. But the business world doesn't stand still, and over time things changed.

If a team has been successful for many years, they will tend to keep doing those things that made them successful, even when those things don't work anymore. When they start to fail, they will tend to blame their failure on everything, and everyone, except themselves. They get to a point where they are in denial and unable to learn.

It's times like these when paying attention is the most important thing you can do.

This is how General David Petraeus operated in Iraq. His helicopters would land with little warning. He would walk in to a situation, and if he did have assumptions, nobody could figure out what they were. He simply observed and asked questions, without letting people know why he was asking or what he thought. There was no way to look at his face and figure out what he wanted to hear.

Why is this important? Typically, when a boss or superior asks a subordinate what's going on, they ask questions like, "How is everything going, soldier? How are you holding up?" By the nature of the question, it's obvious what the boss wants to hear: "Everything's great, sir!"

But when Petraeus asked questions, he didn't give clues about what he wanted to hear. He might have asked questions like "What did you do this morning?" or "When was the last time you had contact with the enemy and what happened?"

Good leaders supplement the information that's coming to them through official channels with a lot of walking around and sense-making on the ground.

This is a very difficult thing to do. Often unconsciously, especially as a leader, you will tend to broadcast what you want to hear, not just by your words, but by your tone, facial expressions, and body language.

This is much harder than it might seem. It takes an open mind and a poker face.

There's an old story about a professor who went to visit a master to learn about Zen. The master poured tea into the professor's cup until it was full, and then kept pouring. The professor watched until he could not restrain himself.

"The cup is full!" he said. "No more will go in!"

"Like this cup," said the master, "your head is full of ideas and opinions. How can I show you Zen unless you first empty your cup?"[1]

EMPTY YOUR CUP

In order to learn anything truly new, you must empty your cup, so your existing knowledge, theories, assumptions, and preconceptions don't get in the way. In Zen practice, this is called *beginner's mind*.

1. Paul Reps, comp., *Zen Flesh, Zen Bones: A Collection of Zen and Pre-Zen Writings* (Rutland, VT: Charles E. Tuttle Co., 1957).

Beginner's mind means that you take on an attitude of openness, curiosity, and eagerness to learn, that you come to a new situation with a blank slate and an open mind, just as a beginner would, even if you are already an expert in a subject.

This is much harder than it would seem. It requires you to suspend disbelief, at least temporarily—to forget things that you know like the back of your hand, to discount things that seem obvious, and to open your mind to ideas that seem strange, absurd, incoherent, and sometimes even impossible.

This opening up of your mind, this willingness to feel dumb, to be vulnerable, to, in effect, rewire your brain in times of change, is the essence of liminal thinking.

Empty your cup.

EXERCISES

- Spend time with someone and try to listen to them as if you were hearing them for the first time. Empty your cup of all your theories and judgments about that person. Take your ego out of it as completely as you can. Listen as if that were your only goal: to listen. See what happens.

- Take 20 minutes out of your day and stop doing anything other than paying attention. Pay attention to your environment, to your surroundings. Pay attention to what people are saying and doing. Notice as much as you can, with all of your senses. Pay attention to your feelings and reactions to what's happening. What do you notice?

Empty your cup.

You can't learn new things
without letting go of old things.
Stop, look, and listen.
Suspend judgment.
What's going on?

It is only with the heart that one can see rightly; what is essential is invisible to the eye.

—Antoine de Saint-Exupéry

3

Create Safe Space

I remember sitting in a meeting some years ago. A major change initiative was about to launch. The CEO said, "Does everyone understand what we're going to do?" Everyone around the table nodded. "Everyone is in agreement. This is the way we're going to do this?" Nods and agreement, all around. "Everyone knows what they are supposed to do, right?" Yep, everyone nodded again. "Okay, let's get started."

What do you think happened next?

Nothing.

Nobody did what they said they were going to do. In fact, some people actively undermined the project, telling peers and subordinates that it was doomed to fail.

Have you ever seen this dynamic at work? I have seen it, many times. Too many to count.

I used to think that good communication was all about clarity and understanding. I named my company XPLANE because we focused on explaining things. The purpose of our company, originally, was to make information crystal-clear, so everyone would know what to do.

I was convinced that the biggest problems of organizational change were complexity and confusion, and that if we could help companies explain things more clearly, their change problems would go away.

Boy, was I wrong.

I've discovered that people will often say they agree when they don't agree. They will say they are on board when they are not on board. They will say that they don't understand something when they understand it perfectly well.

In a top-down organizational hierarchy, "I don't understand" is a polite way of saying "No, I'm not going to do this."

Why does this dynamic play out time and time again, in organizations large and small, all over the world?

It has to do with emotion. Feelings.

We've all heard the saying "leave your emotions at the door." It's a common saying in business. Be objective. Focus on the facts.

Nice idea. Unfortunately, it's not possible.

Emotions are an important and necessary part of the reasoning process. If you had no emotions, no feelings, no needs, then there would never be a reason to do anything.

There would be nothing to be objective about. Everybody has needs. You do the things you do—go to work, go shopping, eat lunch, and so on—in order to meet your needs: your need for food, water, shelter, and once those are met, your need for higher-level things: a nicer house and car, or maybe greater meaning and purpose.

"Leave your emotions at the door" is a dangerous idea. You cannot take off your emotions and leave them at the door, like an overcoat.

I don't mean to suggest that we should go to meetings and act like emotional messes, but we achieve results in life not because we are objective but because we care.

When a meeting, for example, is not a safe place for people to share their feelings and their needs, you will get people saying one thing and doing another, a story we have all seen play out hundreds of times.

Why do people say they agree when they don't agree? Because somebody asked them to leave their emotions at the door, that's why. And when they left the meeting, they put their emotions back on and went back to work.

Reason does not get people to act. *Emotion* is what causes people to act. People can think something is perfectly logical and still not do it because they don't care enough about it, or they don't have any emotional attachment to it. The reason that people do things, especially heroic or major things, things that take a lot of effort, is because they care.

Imagine a basketball team that left their emotions at the door whenever they went into a game. They would never win! If you leave your emotions at the door, what's the point in even playing a game like basketball, what's the point in winning? There is no point.

People will often reveal their beliefs in casual conversation. But people's emotional needs are not easy to uncover.

Why? If I reveal my emotional needs to you, that makes me vulnerable to being manipulated by you. That's not an easy or comfortable place to be. It requires a lot of trust. So if trust is lacking for some reason, people will conceal their needs.

Here's an example. A grocery store chain wanted to launch a web store, so customers could order online and get groceries delivered directly to their homes. They invested a lot of money in this initiative. After some time, the project had stalled, and they didn't know why. Every time they had a meeting, it was packed with store managers. Meeting after meeting, endless discussion, and yet nothing was moving forward. Senior managers could not figure out why the project was stuck.

As it turns out, the problem was that store managers had an emotional need that they were not comfortable expressing or discussing openly.

Their performance was measured, and they got their bonuses, based on in-store sales. If customers ordered online instead of coming into the store, they worried that it would hurt their paycheck. That created a lot of anxiety, but store managers could not openly discuss it, because it would seem like they were not team players.

So instead of openly talking about their fears, they found other ways to stall the project. They expressed concerns about logistics, reliability, storage, and a million other things, instead of being straightforward about their feelings.

Once senior management understood the store managers' fears, they were able to adjust incentives so that sales would be credited to the store managers whether they were in-store or online. The initiative soon was back on track.

Actions and results are observable, beliefs less so.

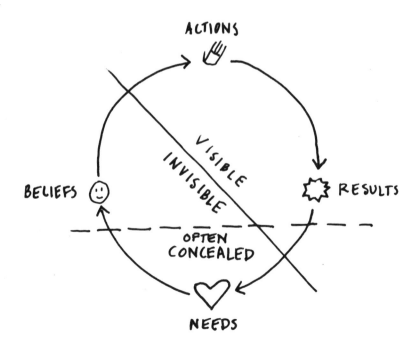

But needs are not only invisible, they are often intentionally hidden, because exposing them makes people feel vulnerable. It can take a bit of digging and detective work to even figure out what they are.

David Rock of the NeuroLeadership Institute has developed a brain-science-based model for thinking about emotional needs, which he calls the SCARF model.[1] SCARF is an acronym that stands for Status, Certainty, Autonomy, Relatedness, and Fairness.

THE SCARF MODEL

If your emotional needs are not being met, the brain reacts in the same way as it would if you were starving. It activates the primary fight-or-flight reactions in the brain. To the brain, at least, emotional needs are as real as physical ones.

The SCARF model is definitely a simplified model, and it's not without limitations. Some would say it's an oversimplification. Nevertheless, I find it helpful because it provides a quick checklist of needs that are easy to remember, and it provides a good set of things to think about

---

1. David Rock, "SCARF: A Brain-Based Model for Collaborating with and Influencing Others," *NeuroLeadership Journal*, Issue 1 (2008).

when you are trying to understand where other people are coming from. Here's a set of questions, based on the SCARF model, which I have found useful.

1. **Status:** Does this person feel important, recognized, or needed by others?

2. **Certainty:** Does this person feel confident that they know what's ahead, and that they can predict the future with reasonable certainty?

3. **Autonomy:** Does this person feel like they have control of their life, their work, and their destiny?

4. **Relatedness:** Does this person feel like they belong? Do they feel a sense of relatedness? Do they trust the group to look after them?

5. **Fairness:** Does this person feel like they are being treated fairly? Do they feel that the "rules of the game" give them a fair chance?

Organizational dynamics expert Esther Derby told me this story:

A call center had a policy that if people worked late, they could take a cab home, because at later hours the buses were no longer running.

One night, after being asked to work an extra shift and getting off at 11 p.m., two people had stopped at the bar across from the office building to have a drink before calling the cab.

The VP of the call center found out about this, and, incensed by this minor breach, she then instituted a policy that any reimbursement over five dollars would need to be personally reviewed by her. Why? A rational person might note that the cab from the bar across the street did not cost the company any more than it would have if the workers went straight home. But the thinking behind the VP's decision was never questioned or explained.

Did that workplace feel safe enough for people to show initiative? I doubt it. This is unfortunately very common. Many, I might even say most, workplaces do not feel safe. They are often rife with politics, gossip, and rumor. Gossip and rumor, by the way, are mostly about stories, and stories tend to be expressions of beliefs. So when people gossip and share rumors, they are weaving a story web. One of the reasons unsafe places tend to feed rumor and gossip is that people are trying to fill that need for safety in a place where it doesn't exist for them.

Here's another story:

My wife, Michelle, used to work at a technology company.

She was working as the communications manager at this company, and the rest of the office was out of town at a conference. She was expected to be in the office that day to make sure that she could take any calls that came in, even though she didn't normally field calls. That morning the temperatures were below zero. She was driving our son to school, and she noticed that the car was not heating. It was just freezing cold, and she smelled something burning. She got our son to school, but the car broke down, and she had to be towed to the garage. I was out of town, unfortunately, so I was no help at all.

So, knowing that she wasn't going to be able to make it to work that day, she called in and left a message for the rest of the team, got a ride home from the guy at the auto shop place, and forwarded all the office calls to her personal cell phone. So she was able to handle everything, just as if she had been in the office.

That wasn't good enough. The next day the boss chewed her out.

He could have said, "Oh, wow, I'm so sorry you got stranded on the highway, but what great initiative. What a good job you did to take care of everything in such difficult circumstances." But he didn't say that.

What he said was, "You didn't have the right to make the decision to work from home without getting my verbal authority. You should have taken a taxi to work and actually been there in person."

How do you think that made her feel? In one fell swoop, he ticked off three out of five SCARF points: he diminished her status, took away her autonomy, and treated her in a way that she felt was unfair.

If you're a boss and you're acting like this, I can guarantee that your best people will be leaving to find other jobs, and you will be left with those who are afraid to leave. They will stay out of fear, because they are afraid they can't get anything better. And that will hurt your company in the long run, which will probably hurt you, too.

Stories like this are all too common. People need to feel that they matter, that they have control over their lives, and that they can make decisions for themselves. They need to feel that they are being treated fairly.

Well, I don't think I have to tell you this, but Michelle doesn't work there anymore, and over time, almost everyone else who was working there at the time has also quit.

When people's basic emotional needs are met, they do better work. When they feel valued and important, they perform at much higher levels. When they have a sense of control, they will take initiative. When they feel a sense of belonging, they will contribute more. When they feel they are being treated fairly, they will go the extra mile.

If you take these things away, you are starving them emotionally. When people are emotionally starving, they come up with conspiracy theories. They cover up, hide, and hoard information. They play political games.

Liminal thinking involves an awareness of the important role that emotional needs play in the formation of beliefs; how beliefs then become habits of action; and how through those actions we create the world we live in.

In any situation where you are dealing with others, especially those situations involving conflict, ask yourself, *do I truly understand the need?*

And don't leave your emotions at the door.

Chris Ortiz is a business analyst who works in large organizations and one of the more effective change agents I know. Here's one simple thing he did to create safe space in a large company.

He simply put an electric tea kettle in his cubicle, and filled the space with lots of different kinds of teacups and all kinds of tea. He created this comfortable place in the middle of a sea of gray cubicles that was attractive, and he would invite people to have tea with him.

The larger company was not a safe-feeling place. At first, people would ask, "Is this allowed? How do you get away with this?" That's how unsafe a place it was.

He would say, "Yeah, it's not a problem, I do it all the time."

Since Chris was involved in major change projects, people would often come to him in the natural course of business, with problems and issues. Sometimes they would be furious.

Chris would say, let's have a cup of tea and talk about this. And, of course, making a cup of tea takes a little time. You have to wait for the water to boil, steep the tea, and so on. So that created a short pause. And he discovered, he told me, that it's impossible to be angry with a warm cup of tea in your hands. I've tried to do it, and I think he's right.

People would come in to talk to him, and they would be hopping mad. He would make some tea and say, "Okay, what's the problem?"

And the answer would come back, "Well, I guess I'm a little calmer now. I can tell you about the problem." And the conversation would move forward.

CREATE SAFE SPACE

What was Chris doing? Is there a method to this madness? Yes, there is. He was carving out *safe space*, space for people to be vulnerable, space where people could safely reveal their anxieties, frustrations, and emotional, unmet needs.

Sharing food and drink is a powerful way to create safe space. Software developer and consultant Linda Rising told me about a project she once worked on where the team was distributed all over the world. There were people on the team from the U.S., Poland, India, and China. Different time zones, different cultures.

Her team was having some problems with the results they were getting, especially in India and China. The team members there were falling behind, and they were reluctant to share bad news. Cultural differences were getting in the way of clear communication. It was hurting the overall project because it was very important for the whole team to know the status of everything that was going on so they could make adjustments if necessary.

Linda shared a cookie recipe with everyone on the team and asked them to make cookies for a scheduled call, so they could all eat the cookies at the same time. The cookies, and, more importantly, the conversation around the cookies, and the memories that were shared, helped to increase the trust between teams, and they were able to resolve their communication problems.

Liminal thinking requires these kinds of safe spaces. It's not possible to have a meaningful dialogue across belief bubbles if people don't feel safe, and safe space requires trust.

Trust has to be earned, and it's not something you can earn in a short period of time. As you can imagine, making cookies is not a quick fix. Making tea in your cubicle is not a quick fix. For Chris and Linda, it was part of a long-term strategy to help them build trust so they could get a better picture of the situation that they were trying to change.

The only way that you can really understand what people's motivations are is to create a space that's safe enough for them to come out of their self-sealing logic bubble, to cultivate curiosity and openness, and to give them a feeling of safety.

CREATE SAFE SPACE

Safe space does not mean that you have to agree with everything that they say. But it does require you to suspend your judgments, at least temporarily. If you want someone to share their real motivations with you, they will need to feel that they're accepted for who they are. They will need to feel respected. They will need to feel that they are not being judged, that they're being treated like a human being, and that even if you don't agree with them, you are at least open to hearing what they have to say.

This can be very difficult, but if you can create that space for other people, you will learn a lot about why they act in the ways that they do. And the more you can understand about that, the more doors of change will open for you.

EXERCISES

- Think back to the last time you had a conflict with someone and use the SCARF model to think through the needs that were involved in that situation. What emotional needs of yours were not being met? What unmet needs do you think they might have had? Think about different ways you might have acted in that situation that might have brought about a different result.

- Think of a place where you feel emotionally safe. What are the things that make it feel safe to you?

  Consider places where you spend time that do not feel emotionally safe, whether it's home, work, or somewhere else. Now compare it to that safe place. What might you do to make that unsafe place feel safer?

Create safe space.

If you don't understand the underlying need, nothing else matters. People will not share their innermost needs unless they feel safe, respected, and accepted for who they are.

A theory that explains everything, explains nothing.

—Karl Popper

4

Triangulate and Validate

Here's a story I heard from a friend of mine named Adrian Howard. His team was working on a software project, and they were working so hard that they were burning themselves out. They were working late nights, and they agreed as a team to slow down their pace. "We're going to work 9 to 5, and we're going to get as much done as we can, but we're not going to stay late. We're not going to work late at night. We're going to pace ourselves. Slow and steady wins the race."

Well, there was one guy on the team who just didn't do that. He was staying late at night, and Adrian was getting quite frustrated by that. Adrian had a theory about what was going on. What seemed obvious to him was that this guy was being macho, trying to prove himself, trying to outdo all the other coders, and showing them that he was a tough guy. Everything that Adrian could observe about this guy confirmed that belief.

Late one night, Adrian was so frustrated that he went over and confronted the guy about the issue. He expected a confrontation, but to his surprise, the guy broke down in tears. Adrian discovered that this guy was not working late because he was trying to prove something, but because home wasn't a safe place for him. They were able to achieve a breakthrough, but it was only possible because Adrian went up and talked to him. Without that conversation, there wouldn't have been a breakthrough.

It's easy to make up theories about why people do what they do, but those theories are often wrong, even when they can consistently and reliably predict what someone will do.

For example, think about your horoscope. Horoscopes make predictions all the time:

> "Prepare yourself for a learning experience about leaping to conclusions."

> "You may find the atmosphere today a bit oppressive."

> "Today, what seems like an innocent conversation will hold an entirely different connotation for one of the other people involved."

> "Stand up to the people who usually intimidate you. Today, they will be no match for you."

These predictions are so vague that you can read anything you want into them. They are practically self-fulfilling prophecies: if you believe them, they are almost guaranteed to come true, because you will set your expectations and act in ways that make them come true. And in any case, they can never be disproven.

So what makes a good theory, anyway?

A scientist and philosopher named Karl Popper spent a lot of time thinking about this. Here's the test he came up with, and I think it's a good one: Does the theory make a prediction that might not come true? That is, can it be proven false?

What makes this a good test? Popper noted that it's relatively easy to develop a theory that offers predictions—like a horoscope—that can never be disproven.

The test of a good theory, he said, is not that it *can't* be disproven, but that it *can* be disproven.

For example, if I have a theory that you are now surrounded by invisible, undetectable, flying elephants, well, there's no way you can prove me wrong. But if my theory can be subjected to some kind of test—if it is possible that it could be disproved, then the theory can be tested.

He called this trait *falsifiability*: the possibility that a theory could be proven false.

Many theories people have about other people are like horoscopes. They are not falsifiable theories, but self-fulfilling prophecies that can never be disproven.

Just because you can predict someone's behavior does not validate your theories about them, any more than a horoscope prediction "coming true" means it was a valid prediction. If you want to understand what's going on inside someone else's head, sometimes you need to have a conversation with them.

Many years after the Vietnam War, former U.S. Secretary of Defense Robert McNamara met with Nguyen Co Thach, former Foreign Minister of Vietnam, who had fought for the Viet Cong in the war. McNamara had formed the hypothesis that the war could have been avoided, that Vietnam and the United States could have both achieved their objectives without the terrible loss of life. When he presented his thinking to Thach, Thach said, "You're totally wrong. We were fighting for our independence. You were fighting to enslave us."

"But what did you accomplish?" asked McNamara. "You didn't get any more than we were willing to give you at the beginning of the war. You could have had the whole damn thing: independence, unification."

"Mr. McNamara," answered Thach. "You must have never read a history book. If you had, you'd know that we weren't pawns of the Chinese or the Russians. Don't you understand that we have been fighting the Chinese for a thousand years? We were fighting for our independence. And we would fight to the last man. And we were determined to do so. And no amount of bombing, no amount of U.S. pressure would ever have stopped us."[1]

McNamara then realized that the entire war had been based on a complete misunderstanding. He said: "In the case of Vietnam, we didn't know them well enough to empathize. And there was total misunderstanding as a result. They believed that we had simply replaced the French as a colonial power, and we were seeking to subject South and North Vietnam to our colonial interests, which was absolutely absurd. And we saw Vietnam as an element of the Cold War. Not what they saw it as: a civil war."[2]

Sometimes people come into conflict not because they disagree, but because they fundamentally misunderstand each other. This can happen when people are viewing a situation from completely different points of view.

Have you ever had someone that you worked with, where you thought, this person is insane; they make no sense; they are crazy; they're just nuts?

---

1. *The Fog of War: Eleven Lessons from the Life of Robert McNamara*, documentary directed by Erroll Morris (Sony Pictures, 2003).
2. Ibid.

Everyone knows someone like that, right?

Sometimes people really do have mental disorders, including problems that can create danger for themselves and others. If that's the case, it might make sense to stay away from them, or to seek help from a mental health professional.

But far more often, saying another person is crazy is just a way to create internal coherence within your belief bubble. Your "obvious" is stopping you from seeing clearly. The "crazy person" may be acting based on beliefs that are inconceivable to you because they are outside your bubble.

If you think to yourself, this person is just nuts, and nothing can be done about it, it can't be changed, then it's possible that your theory about that person is constrained by a limiting belief.

Most people don't test their theories about other people, because it's a potential bubble-buster: if you give your self-sealing logic bubble a true test, then it just might collapse on you.

People do fake tests all the time, of course.

Here's an easy way to do a fake test of your beliefs. Just search the Internet. No matter what your belief is, you'll find plenty of articles that support and reinforce your bubble. The Internet is like a grocery store for facts. It's easier than ever to find "facts" that support pretty much any belief.

Fake tests will help if your goal is to feel better about yourself and reinforce your bubble. But if you want to figure out what is really going on, a fake test will not help.

What will help is triangulation: the practice of developing multiple viewpoints and theories that you can compare, contrast, combine, and validate, to get a better understanding of what's going on.

U.S. military strategist Roy Adams told me this story about an "aha" moment he had in Iraq.

He was having a beer with a friend who was in the Special Forces. Usually, they didn't talk about work, but he happened to have a map with him. At the time, Adams and his team were designing their plans based on the political boundaries of the map, so on the map were districts, as well as the people who were in charge of the districts.

His friend said, "You know, this is really interesting." And he picked up a pen and said, "Let me draw the tribal boundaries on this map for you." The boundaries were completely different but overlapping. Suddenly, Adams had two different versions of reality on his map.

The political map was primarily a Shia map, and the tribal map had both Sunni and Shia. Only by overlaying the two maps did Adams start to understand the situation. Neither map would have made sense by itself.

By laying these maps over each other, suddenly things started to click. Now he understood why they were having success in some places and meeting resistance in others. Everything started to make more sense.

The insights in this case came not from one map or another, but through overlaying them. This is the practice of triangulation. Each map represented one theory of the world, one version of reality. It was only by viewing the situation through multiple perspectives—multiple theories— that he was able to gain insight and see the situation differently.

LOOK FOR ALTERNATIVES

My friend Adrian Howard told me about a similar experience he had when working at a large Telecom company that had grown by acquiring other companies over many years. His team found itself running up against resistance and pushback that seemed odd and inexplicable. Then someone on the team took some markers and color-coded the boxes on the org chart based on which companies the people in each box had originally come from—many of whom used to be fierce competitors—and suddenly the reasons for the resistance became clear and understandable.

For any one observation there may be a vast number of possible explanations. Many of them may be based on beliefs that are outside of your current belief bubble, in which case, they may seem strange, absurd, crazy, or just plain wrong.

Most of the time we are all walking around with our heads so full of "obvious" that we can't see what's really going on. If you think something is obvious, that's an idea that bears closer examination. Why do you think it's obvious? What personal experiences have you had that led to that belief? Can you imagine a different set of experiences that might lead to a different belief?

Cultivate as many theories as you can—including some that seem odd, counterintuitive, or even mutually contradictory—and hold onto them loosely. Don't get too attached to any one of them.

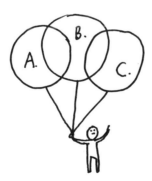

HOLD YOUR THEORIES
LOOSELY

Then you can start asking questions and seeking valid information to help you understand what's really going on. The way to seek understanding is to empty your cup, step up and give people your full attention, suspend your beliefs and judgments, and listen carefully.

The thing to remember is that people act in ways that make sense to them. If something doesn't make sense to you, then you're missing something.

What are you missing? If someone says something that seems odd or unbelievable, ask yourself, "What would I need to believe for that to be true?"

In many cases, the only way you're ever going to understand what's inside someone else's head is by talking to them. Sometimes that idea might seem scary. It may be that you will hear something that threatens your bubble of belief. But if you can get over your fear, go and talk to the dragon, or take the ogre out for coffee. You just may learn something that will change your life.

EXERCISES

- Think about a co-worker or family member, someone you care about, or can't walk away from for whatever reason, that you have trouble getting along with. Consider their beliefs and behavior, and come up with as many theories as you can to explain why they act the way they do. Then see if you can have a conversation with that person to explore what's really going on.

- Think of a situation at home or work that you find problematic. Try to come up with as many perspectives as you can that might give you a different way to look at the situation. What is your current theory? What is its opposite? How many perspectives or points of view can you think of that might help you see that situation through different eyes?

Triangulate and validate.

Look at situations from as many points of view as possible. Consider the possibility that seemingly different or contradictory beliefs may be valid. If something doesn't make sense to you, then you're missing something.

The greatest compliment that was ever paid me was when one asked me what I thought, and attended to my answer.

—Henry David Thoreau

5

Ask Questions, Make Connections

Mitchell Sipus is a humanitarian aid worker and consultant who has worked in some of the world's most conflict-laden environments: Ethiopia, Lebanon, Somalia, Syria, and Afghanistan.

He was hired by the mayor of Mogadishu, the capital of Somalia, to help solve some of the city's problems. Mitch does a lot of exploring and observation when he enters into something like this. He immerses himself in the situation.

Among other things, he simply walks around and asks people questions, like:

"How do you feel about your life?"

"Is it everything you wanted it to be?"

"If not, why not?"

"What do you think is your biggest obstacle?"

"What would you like to do in the future?"

"What do you think you need to do that?"

What Mitch is doing is trying to understand not just what's going on, but how people see things. He is trying to understand their needs, their beliefs—trying to get a breakdown of everyone's hopes, dreams, and frustrations.

Here's a story about how Mitch operates.

He was hired by the Mayor of Mogadishu, the capital of Somalia, to help solve some of the city's problems. He was wandering around Mogadishu, asking questions like the ones above, and he came across some fishermen. So he asked them his questions, and they told him, "Well, the fishing is great. We are catching more fish than ever before. We're drowning in fish. But we are still not making any money."

"Why not?" he asked.

"Well, we take the fish to the fish market, and there's no refrigeration there, so the fish sit out in the sun all day, and at the end of the day, if nobody buys them, we have to discount the fish to the cheapest price possible, and we practically have to give them away. We don't make any money. Of course, everybody knows this, so they just wait. They don't even show up at the fish market until the end of the day. So we have a problem here."

So Mitch said thank you, and he filed that away and kept exploring.
A few days later, he was walking in another part of the city, and he got
himself some lemonade in a can and started to drink it. There was ice in
the can. He thought, wait a minute, there's no electricity in this part of
town either, so how can there be ice?

He went back to the lemonade stand, and they told him how to find the
guy they got the ice from. And he found this guy who was selling ice.
He had rigged up some machinery and with gas-powered generators
and using giant sarcophagus-sized containers, he was making huge
refrigerator-sized blocks of ice, which he was selling.

So Mitch said to him, "How would you like to expand your business?
To sell more ice? What would you need in order to do that?"

And the guy said, "yeah, sure," and within a short period of time there
was ice in the fish market, and electric lights, too, thanks to this guy.
That is how Mitch works his change magic, by wandering around,
asking questions and connecting the dots.

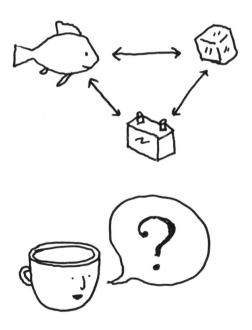

Because he is coming in from outside the system, when Mitch wanders around he will tend to ask questions about things that may seem "obvious" to the people who live in that system. Because of his outside perspective, he can sometimes notice things that insiders don't, or see familiar things in new ways.

By asking people for their hopes, dreams, fears, and frustrations, Mitch is looking to reveal the latent needs and goals of the people in the system—a kind of ecosystem of needs and solutions.

By asking questions, Mitch finds liminal, in-between spaces that people may not have seen or considered. Then, by finding possible intersections between needs and solutions, and forming new connections, he creates new opportunities that were already latent in the system, just waiting to be discovered.

EXERCISE

Try asking Mitch's questions in some area of your social life. How do you feel about your life? Is it everything you wanted it to be? If not, why not? What do you think is your biggest obstacle? What would you like to do in the future? What do you think you need to do that? Can you connect the dots to create new opportunities?

Ask questions, make connections.

Try to understand people's hopes, dreams, and frustrations. Explore the social system and make connections to create new opportunities.

Always remember, your focus
determines your reality.

— George Lucas

6

Disrupt Routines

Here's a story that comes from a book about family therapy.[1]

A couple were having problems with their teenage son. He was being defiant and belligerent. The parents tried to curtail his behavior, but the harder they came down on him, the more defiant he got. They were to the point where they were going to start calling the police, that's how bad it was. It was a classic doom loop.

---

1. Paul Watzlawick, John H. Weakland, Richard Fisch, and Milton H. Erikson, *Change: Principles of Problem Formation and Problem Resolution* (New York: W.W. Norton & Company, 1974).

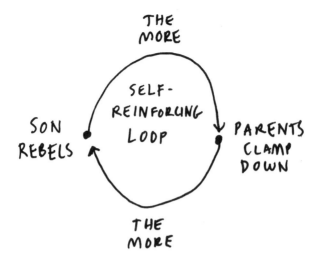

One of the things that was happening was that he would stay out late at night.

The therapist told them, "Here's what I want you to do. I want you to tell him, 'Look, we'd like you to be home by ten, but we realize there is nothing we can do about it. But we'd really like you to be home by ten.'

"And when he doesn't get home by ten, lock the doors, turn out the lights, and go to bed. Don't wait up.

"Then, when he does eventually come home, let him knock or ring the doorbell for a while, and then come down after a bit and open the door. At first, act really sleepy, pretend that you don't recognize him, and then recognize him, and just apologize, say, 'Oh, sorry, son, I'm so sorry, come on in,' and then just go back to bed like it's no big deal.

"If he doesn't make his bed, I want you to make his bed for him, but spill crackers in it or something like that, and if later he complains about the crackers, just say, 'Oh, I'm sorry, son, I was eating crackers when I made your bed and some of them must have gotten in there.'"

What was going on? The therapist realized that the parent's "solution" of clamping down on the kid was just making the problem worse. The son was rebelling against their authority. Taking away the authority—in a way that didn't really make him happy—left the son with nothing to rebel against. If he wanted to get in the house without trouble, he would need to get home on time. If he didn't want crackers in his bed, he needed to make it, and so on.

The parents had a belief: That the son was out of control, and the solution was to reassert control. In order to change the situation, they needed to change their belief that by asserting control they would help their son learn self-control. They needed to get outside the situation and look at how they were influencing it.

Sometimes, the solution makes the problem worse; that's when you get a real conundrum. What do you do? You have to step outside the problem, and then you have to start looking at the solution as well as the problem; and often, the answer to solving that problem is not attacking the problem, itself, but *attacking the solution.*

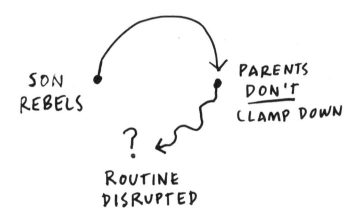

We spend so much time on autopilot. Sometimes, when a problem seems intractable, there's an invisible routine at work, and simply disrupting that routine, even in random ways, can shift the situation and allow you to see it in new ways.

As I've been writing this book I have been sharing the draft with my wife, Michelle, and she has been putting the principles to work at home. She told me this story about disrupting routines.

Our son Isaac has been spending a lot of time playing video games, and it has become a problem that sometimes distracts him from doing his homework or keeps him up late at night.

One night as she was going to bed, she heard Isaac in his room playing a game online with friends. She thought, "Okay, what is my typical, auto-pilot routine?"

Her typical pattern would be to knock on the door and go in there, telling him to stop playing and go to bed. This invariably would end in a fight. So she decided to disrupt that routine and see what happened.

She went downstairs and unplugged the Wi-Fi router. Once in a while, it conks out all on its own, and the only way to restart it is to unplug it and plug it back in. Then she waited there, in the dark, next to the router.

Isaac came down and walked toward the router to restart it, and when he saw her there, after an initial shock, he got it immediately. He just looked at her, then down at the floor. He said, "Sorry," turned around and went right back upstairs to bed.

What happened there? She was disrupting a typical pattern not by attacking the problem, but by attacking her typical *solution* to the problem. The disruption of their typical pattern changed the dynamic completely.

Sometimes a routine is so ingrained and habitual that it has become embedded in the physical environment, and is almost invisible.

Here's an example.

Hunter Industries is a company that makes irrigation and sprinkler systems that are driven by software. The software developers at Hunter Industries worked in cubicles and when they wanted to have a meeting, they needed to book a meeting room. Meeting rooms at Hunter Industries were at a premium, so you were not allowed to book them for more than two hours. Sounds pretty basic, right? Not unreasonable.

A guy named Woody Zuill was brought into Hunter Industries to manage that software team. When he first arrived at Hunter, Woody noticed that his team was stressed out, and they were spending a lot of time in meetings. They were having meetings on top of meetings, and even with all those meetings, the software, which was pretty complex, was breaking a lot. So whenever something broke, they would need to have even more meetings to figure out what was going on.

Woody disrupted the routine, but in a very small way. He is a very collaborative guy and not a top-down manager, so he started making time for the team to reflect and think about their problems, asking them what they thought they should do, and doing his best to make it possible.

One of the things they did was to institute a kind of weekly learning time, where on Friday afternoons they would book a meeting room, with a laptop and a projector, and people would show each other the things that they knew. They would pass the laptop back and forth. It was a nice way to spend a Friday afternoon, and the team members were learning a lot from each other.

One Friday the team got together to meet about a large, complex project they were working on, and they started to talk about the project and who needed to do what, but pretty soon they started passing the laptop back and forth like they did in their weekly learning meetings. After an hour and a half, their meeting time was up, someone else was coming in for another meeting, and they all looked at each other and said, "Well, we're not done yet, so let's book another meeting room."

So they booked another room and kept on with their meeting. It was actually turning into a kind of working meeting, because they were not just talking to each other, they were actually making progress on the project at the same time. They continued like this for the rest of the day, going from meeting room to meeting room and moving the project forward together.

The next week, Woody blocked out meeting rooms all day, every day, and the team was literally going from room to room, meeting and working, and getting a lot done at the same time. After a week of this, they figured it was time to get a room where they could do this permanently.

It took them about three weeks to find a room where they could keep working like this, and now they do it this way pretty much all the time.

So what happened there?

There was a tacit, unspoken, underlying belief that permeated the entire company: the idea that "meeting is not working." This belief was so habitual and embedded that it had been built into the routines and even the physical structure of work, in the form of cubicles, which were "for work," and meeting rooms, which were "for meetings" and needed to be booked and scheduled.

By creating space for reflection, Woody disrupted that routine. At the same time, he created a safe space for learning and reflection, a kind of playful space, which opened up some wiggle room for a new way of working to emerge—a way of working that combined meetings and work into a single activity.

In one sense, they are meeting all the time. They are always in a meeting. But in another sense, they have done away with meetings altogether, because they are always working, too.

The results have been so dramatic that Woody is now in demand all over the world, where he teaches people this new way of working, which he has dubbed "mob programming."

Life is full of these kinds of patterns and routines. Over time they become invisible.

Think about your route to work. If you're like me, you take that trip on autopilot. You take the same route every day, so you see the same things, and over time it gets to the point where you don't even notice them. But if there is construction or something and that road is blocked, you are forced to find a new way, and you are inevitably going to pay attention in new ways and notice new things.

You can do this intentionally in other parts of your life as well. Whenever you find yourself stuck in any kind of recurring pattern, try something random. Anything you can do that throws that train off the rails will create new openings and might help you see the whole situation in a new way. Just do something different.

EXERCISES

- Think of a relationship in your life where you have a recurring doom loop pattern. Find a way to disrupt that routine, even if it's random. See what happens.

- Talk to someone you usually wouldn't talk to. Go to a place you wouldn't usually go. Disrupt yourself. Change it up. Do something different.

Disrupt routines.

Many beliefs are embedded in habitual routines that run on autopilot. Disrupt the routine to create new possibilities.

Action may not always bring happiness, but there is no happiness without action.

—William James

7

Act As If in the Here and Now

Jason Roberts was an IT consultant living in Dallas. He got back to Dallas after visiting Europe, and he said to himself, "Everywhere I went in Europe they have these big beautiful plazas with pigeons and street vendors and all these wonderful things. Why don't we have that in Dallas? Why don't we have that in my neighborhood? Why do we just have giant freeway ramps and big empty spaces?"

If he hadn't been a change agent, he might have left it at that.

But he thought, I want to see what I saw in Europe, but I want to see it happening here, in my hometown. I want more of that feeling.

The first thing he did was go to the city council to see what the laws were. And he found that there were all kinds of arcane rules that made it very difficult to do anything. For example, you had to pay a thousand dollars for a license if you wanted to have outdoor tables. That looks like an obstacle, right? Most people would see it that way.

But he just said, we're going to get a group of people together, friends, and we're going to set up a kind of temporary neighborhood design, and we're going to break as many of these rules as we possibly can, and then we're going to invite the city council down and we're going to show them what could happen, and then we're going to ask them, "Why do we have all these rules?"

And that's exactly what they did. They kind of swarmed over a neighborhood and got everyone involved, and they made a vacant lot into a park, and they narrowed the street and widened the walking space by blocking off a couple of street lanes with big planters, and they made a sidewalk café. They painted a crosswalk on the street. It was a completely guerilla pop-up urban scenario.

There was a conflict between the rules and what they wanted to see happening. So, they just surfaced the conflict and made it very visible, by acting as if those obstacles didn't exist. They created, in a temporary way, a possible, parallel world, a prototype of a potential city, one that was unconstrained by the existing rules.

They invited the city council members to see what they had done, and they asked the question, "Why do we have all these rules?"

And the city council people said, "We actually don't know why all these rules exist. Some of them are hundreds of years old, and we can change them. We don't need them."

The constraints were imaginary. They were just old rules, and nobody even knew why they were there.

This is the secret of challenging existing beliefs. If you can form a hypothesis, you don't have to necessarily believe it's true in order to test it. You can simply act as if it were true and see what happens.

Let's go back to the learning loop for a second. This is the typical way we learn about the world and improve our beliefs and behavior over time.

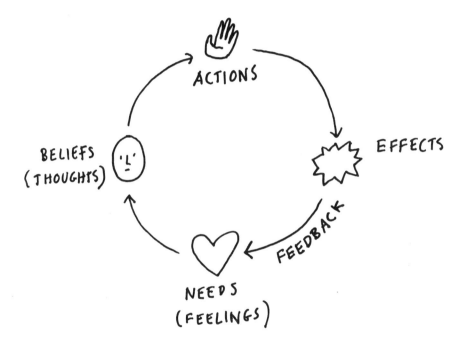

SINGLE-LOOP LEARNING

ACTIONS

EFFECTS

FEEDBACK

NEEDS
(FEELINGS)

BELIEFS
(THOUGHTS)

The single loop works in most circumstances, because you are building on your existing experiences, refining, honing, and polishing your existing, mostly successful beliefs.

But there are times when a belief no longer works, or it isn't enough. You are stuck, and getting unstuck feels like it's unlikely or impossible. You need a new approach.

That's when you need double-loop learning.

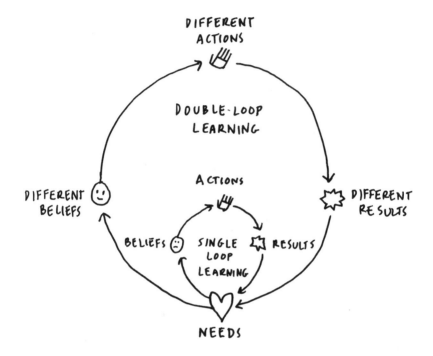

Double-loop learning is a way to break out of a rut by challenging your own beliefs and trying on new ones. You can even test beliefs that you think are wrong—and you should.

It's a bit like Zen Buddhism. A Zen Buddhist will tell you, "You don't have to believe anything in particular to reach enlightenment. You just have to sit."

In the case of double-loop learning, you don't have to believe a hypothesis in order to test it. All you have to do is act as if it were true and see what happens. Ask yourself, "How would I act if I believed this were true?"

Change is only possible in the here-and-now, and the way to create change is by acting in the here-and-now as if a different world existed. For example, act as if the world you want to create is already here.

CHANGE IS ONLY
POSSIBLE IN THE
HERE-AND-NOW

Here's how to practice double-loop learning:

1. First, recognize that, although you may not be able to see it, you are operating in a bubble of belief, a reality distortion field.

2. Don't just observe behavior. Try to figure out the underlying needs and beliefs that are operating in any situation you want to change.

3. Are you seeing the results that you want? If so, great!

4. If not, explore and examine as many alternative beliefs as you can. Expose yourself—or your team—to more ideas and experiences. Search for a belief that looks interesting and act as if it were true for a period of time.

5. See what happens. Did you improve the situation? If so, great! If not, repeat as necessary.

There are worlds of possibility all around you—many possible ways to operate, many possible beliefs. With each set of beliefs comes a new set of possibilities. You won't know what the range of those possibilities look like until you begin to explore them.

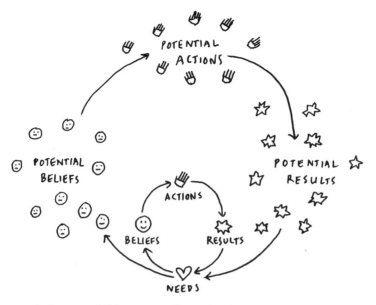

LIMINAL OPPORTUNITIES ARE ALL AROUND YOU
EXPLORE THE POSSIBILITIES

Double-loop learning is a powerful tool because it gives you a way to test new ideas that you would otherwise ignore or discount, because they are coming from outside your existing bubble. You don't have to actually believe something is true in order to test it. All you have to do is *act as if it were true* and see what happens.

EXERCISES

- Pick an area of your life where you would like to see positive change. Make a list of your beliefs about that situation. For each belief on the list, make a list of alternative beliefs. They don't have to be things you actually think are true, just things that might possibly be true. Make sure you put a few absurd things on the list. Now, pick a belief that looks interesting and act as if it were true for a period of time. See what happens.

- Make a list of things in your life that you are happy with and that are going well. How might you turn up the good?

Act as-if in the here-and-now.

You can test beliefs even if you don't believe they are true.

All you need to do is act as if they were true and see what happens.

If you find something that works, do more of it.

How could you live and have no story to tell?

—Fyodor Dostoyevsky

8

Make Sense with Stories

I was in a taxi with the CEO and the head of sales. It was sort of an accident that I was in the taxi. It just so happened that we were all heading to the airport about the same time.

The executives were deeply involved in a conversation that I wouldn't have usually heard. I was in the front seat, and they were in the back. They were talking about sales numbers.

It became evident to me that they were explaining the sales numbers to themselves using self-sealing logic. They were simply looking at the numbers and making up stories to explain why the sales weren't happening.

This guy isn't stepping up to the plate. That person dropped the ball. This person is incompetent. I knew enough about the situation to realize that these stories they were telling each other were pure fantasy.

I said, "Have you talked to the customer? What about talking to the customer?"

What do you think they said? Do you have a guess?

They didn't say a thing. They just paused in their conversation, and after a moment they just went right back to their fantasy conversation.

That's how powerful self-sealing logic is.

This is so common. People ask, "Why isn't this happening?" and instead of going out and exploring, trying to find valid information, they make up stories.

I've been telling a lot of stories in this book. Story after story. Every chapter starts with a story. Why am I telling all these stories?

I started out this book by explaining that a belief is a story in your head. Stories are one of the primary ways we make sense of experiences. To share those experiences later, we tell a story. When people tell stories, they are not just sharing knowledge, but building relationships and expressing beliefs.

Why stories? Facts alone may provide information, but a story gives you context that connects those facts to people, situations, and events. It gives them meaning. Give people facts without a story, and they will create a story to make sense of the facts.

Stories are learning tools. Since language began, a story was the best way to share an experience so that others could learn from it.

In fact, a good story works like a drug, releasing hormones in the brains of the teller and listeners. Brain scans show that when people share stories with each other, their brains connect and mirror each other. Their neurons literally fire in the same pattern in a phenomenon known as *neural coupling*.

When people hear a stressful, dramatic, high point of a story, their brain releases cortisol, the same hormone that creates the fight-or-flight response and creates strong memories of emotional experiences. And when conflicts or difficulties are resolved, the brain releases oxytocin, the hormone released by physical touch, which creates social bonds and feelings of contentment, calm, and security.[1]

When someone tells you a story, they are sharing an experience and expressing their beliefs about that experience at the same time. In addition, both teller and listener are pairing their brains, building relationships and creating social cohesion that makes it easier for them to develop shared goals and move toward those goals in a collaborative, coordinated way.

THE BEST WAY TO
SHARE A BELIEF IS
WITH A STORY

Prompting other people to tell stories, and listening to them, is as much of an art as storytelling. When you ask someone to tell a story, you are telling them that their experiences are important, that they have meaning, and that they matter.

1. Paul Zak, *The Moral Molecule: The Source of Love and Prosperity* (New York: Dutton Adult, 2012).

A good way to elicit stories from people is through the use of something called a *story prompt*. Story prompts are questions about people's experiences and how they made meaning out of them. Things like:

> "Think of the best team you've ever been a part of. What happened that made you feel that way?"

> "What is the most scared you have ever been? What happened?"

> "Tell me about a time when you felt uncomfortable or out of place. What did you do about it?"

> "What was your best day at work here, and what made it great?"

> "What was your worst day, and what happened that made it so bad?"

> "Did you ever have an experience that changed your life? What happened?"

When you ask someone to tell you a story, you are inviting them to deepen their connection with you, to bond with you. It's an invitation that says their life and experiences are important, meaningful, and worth learning from. It's a simple step you can take, every day, to create a shared world with the people who matter to you.

Every good story starts with a person in some kind of situation: a problem, a choice, or an opportunity. Then the story tells you what they did, and why, and then it tells you what happened because of that. Maybe a lesson was learned. If the story is good enough, it's worth remembering and repeating to others.

This makes a story a **perfect mechanism** for making sense of, and sharing, information. **In effect, a story translates facts into** "rules for action." A story is just **about the most perfect** way to package and share beliefs that you will ever find.

Listen to the stories someone tells, notice the stories they respond to most positively, and you will begin to understand their beliefs—and their bubble.

If you have beliefs that you want to share, beliefs that you think may change the world for the better, the way to help those beliefs take flight is to share them as stories.

EXERCISES

- Make a list of some of your favorite stories. What are some stories you find yourself telling about yourself and your life, over and over? What does that tell you about your beliefs?

- Think about your friends, family members, and co-workers. What stories do they tell? What do those stories say about their beliefs?

Make sense with stories.

If you give people facts without a story, they will explain it within their existing belief system.
The best way to promote a new or different belief is not with facts, but with a story.

If you can change your mind,
you can change your life.

—William James

9

Evolve Yourself

My friend Chris Ortiz works on big change projects. The guy who makes tea, remember?

He was working on a project at a company where the CEO was a former military man, and there was a kind of unwritten rule that everyone in the company would wear white shirts and blue pants or skirts.

It looked like the marines, he told me, when you went to work.

What did he do? What's the one small thing that he did to act as if a different world were possible?

He didn't follow the unwritten dress code. He just ignored it. Just one small poke to the story web that defined that company.

He would wear nice clothes, but not blue pants and not a white shirt. It seems like a very small change, doesn't it? It was a tiny, little thing.

He also set up a whiteboard in his cubicle, and every morning he would draw a different picture on it. Palm trees, flowers, just whatever came into his head that morning. Something happy.

What happened? I'll bet you can guess. People started coming up to him, asking "How do you get away with that? How do you get away with not following the dress code?"

"I just do it," he would reply.

And they would say things like, "Yeah, but I could never get away with that."

You may think I'm going to say that suddenly there was a dress code revolution. No. That's not the way these things work. But when you challenge a status quo like that, even in tiny ways, it changes things. Disrupting routines starts to shift the patterns of behavior, but not always in ways that you can predict in advance.

Nobody else changed their dress code. Nobody.

But what did happen was that people started to think of Chris as the creative guy in the company. You know, that creative guy in the tech building who doesn't follow the dress code and draws stuff on his cube wall.

And when people ran into a problem, when they got stuck on something, somebody would say, "Maybe we should talk to that creative guy. Maybe he might have some ideas or something."

Soon, he started to get pulled into all of the biggest problems and conflicts that people were dealing with in the company, which it just so happens were also the biggest opportunities for change.

And since he was able to really contribute and help people solve problems, he got a reputation as a problem-solver and was able to make a really big impact.

And all this started just because he changed his clothes.

Change is a tricky thing. It's all around us, all the time, but so much of the time it seems like change controls us, when we really would like it to be the other way around. We all want more control over the changes that impact our lives.

I'm so glad you found this book. I'm even happier that you read this far. It tells me that you want to change things: yourself, your life, and maybe the world.

I don't think it's possible, by the way, to change the world without changing yourself.

You can do it. You can change your life and maybe you can change the world. But I don't want to pretend you can do any of this without taking some risks.

You have probably heard of Intuit, the company that makes QuickBooks, as well as personal finance and tax software. There was a team at Intuit that was selling enterprise accounting software. This product was sold at multiple tiers: you could buy different numbers of licenses at different price points. The more licenses you bought, the lower your cost per license.

The team wondered what would happen if they created a version of the product that was only available under one type of license. They thought that simplifying pricing might increase sales.

The team did some customer research. They talked with some customers and got very positive feedback. They thought they saw a business opportunity and took their idea to the executive team.

The executive team did not share their enthusiasm. They said, "There is no way that would work. These are enterprise customers; they will never buy this."

The team pointed to the fact that customers had actually said that they want this. The executive team said, "We all know that customers say one thing and they do something else. Sorry, this won't work."

The team then decided to run a simple experiment to test their idea. One of the team members had a friend who was working in tele-sales, where many of the enterprise license deals were being made. The team member called in a personal favor and had the tele-sales agent take one hour and add an option to their sales pitch offering the single price point.

The team was surprised at the results of this experiment. Not only had they sold several licenses at the single price point, but there had also been zero impact on the other sales.

These results were almost unbelievable, even to the team. So they double-checked it. They ran the experiment again. The results were still very promising.

Armed with this new evidence, they went back to the executive team and pitched their idea again, this time with quantitative evidence and financial projections.

The executives' reaction this time was completely different. They were excited. They said, "Why hasn't anybody thought of this before?"

The single-license option is now live and responsible for a very large portion of that product's revenue, delivering well beyond any of the smaller changes that were on the previous roadmap.[1]

I love this story because it's the story of a team who cared enough to take a risk. They had the courage to subvert the goals of the organization for an hour or two in order to serve a larger goal.

---

1. This story comes from a talk by Alissa Briggs, "How to Coach Enterprise Experimentation." I heard her talk at the Enterprise UX Conference, San Antonio, Texas, 2015.

STAY FLEXIBLE ABOUT OUTCOMES

There are big risks and small risks. Breaking the dress code is a relatively small risk. It's very unlikely that breaking the dress code will get you fired. You might get embarrassed, or you might get scolded or something, but fired? Probably not. It's a risk, yes, but it's a tiny risk. I broke the dress code at work once (it was one of those unwritten rules), and all that happened was that my boss asked me to go home and change.

It's better to ask forgiveness than permission, but you probably don't need either one.

Asking a tele-sales agent to sell a fictional product is a slightly bigger risk. But it opened up a huge opportunity for the company, and the team was rewarded. And if the experiment had failed, nobody probably would have noticed. It was a calculated risk and one the team thought was worth taking.

Risks come in all shapes and sizes. But risk is there whether you are aware of it or not, and it's important to consider the risks you are taking in any kind of change work.

Detaching yourself from your personal objectives helps you keep the bigger picture in mind. You can't always have things your way. People need to believe that you have good intentions, and that you are looking out for the good of the whole, not just yourself. If people understand that, they are more likely to trust you and to cut you some slack.

So how will your change story end?

The change can succeed, of course, or the change can fail. But there's also often an in-between kind of ending. You made some progress, but you didn't get everything you wanted. Or the situation changed, and it got better in a different way than you intended. Progress, but not perfection. That's what happens with change efforts, one of those three things.

But what about you? There are different ways it can end for you, too.

One is that you stick around. You stay in the organization or the group. Either the change happens, or it doesn't, or it happens in a small way, and you decide to stick it out, remain part of that community and continue to help it grow. That is one ending.

Two is that you go. You learned something interesting, maybe, and it gave you some great idea, and you go out and start a new company, or you go to another job where you feel you have a better chance of achieving your vision. That is another possible ending.

There's a third way it can end, though, and that is you don't stay or go, but remain in liminal territory, on the threshold. That means somehow, you, like me, have become so in love with the change process and seeing things happen that you just want to do it over and over. You become a teacher, or a coach, or a consultant—someone who helps others transform. Not totally on the inside, but not totally outside either. Right there on the threshold.

I once quit my job and turned my old boss into my first customer on the same day. That kind of thing is not only possible, but it happens all the time. People are fired, or they quit, and within a week they are back, working for the old company, as vendors or consultants.

The thing to remember is that no matter how it ends, you are building your own personal capability for change, and you are creating your future. You are contributing to create a future that you want.

Risk is a thing. Risk is real. Fear is a thing, too. I think the biggest barrier for most people is fear. That fear of getting fired, or of losing your job. Change is a risky business. Sometimes your change efforts can create risks for others as well.

You get fired. It happens sometimes. It's happened to me. But, far more often, I've been rewarded or promoted for the risks I've taken, and what I have realized over time is that most of the constraints that keep you from making change happen exist only in your own mind.

If you can learn to be flexible in your own mind about which of those endings happens, if you can avoid becoming too attached to any one of them, and keep them all in play in your mind, it becomes easier to start poking, start exploring, and pushing the boundaries of that bubble to see what's possible. If you're open to any of those possible endings, you can have dramatic success.

Imagine a child in a room, with building blocks spread all over the floor. She plays with the blocks, trying out various ways of combining them to create structures. At first the structures are simple, but over time they become more and more elaborate. By combining and recombining blocks, through trial and error and many experiments, the child creates order from chaos. At some point, she is satisfied: the blocks are combined to make a beautiful and elegant city, with bridges, parks, roads, and happy people. But whether it's a city of the imagination or a real one, there is a point where order is no longer the solution: it is the problem. Unless some degree of chaos is permitted to enter the system, no further progress can be made. Sometimes, to create new structures, the old ones must be destroyed so the blocks can be recombined in different ways.

The mind is similar.

We start, as babies, with a chaos of perceptions, needs, and emotions, like building blocks strewn around a room. From these basic building blocks, we create order. As children, we adopt and discard beliefs on an ongoing basis, pretty easily. Over time and with a lot of experimentation, we create elaborate structures of meaning, beautiful cities of the mind. We create elegant structures of belief, that frame and explain our surroundings, help us make sense of the world, and guide our actions. As these belief structures evolve, and as we act on them, we become more invested in them and more reluctant to throw them away.

At the end of the day, we are dependent on our experiences. They are the most concrete facts of our lives. We assemble this chaotic stream of sensations and perceptions to make order and sense of things. But the world is not static or stable, and the structures of belief that help us navigate our world must evolve continually if we are to remain on top of things. No matter how elaborate or perfect your system of belief may seem, it is vulnerable to the steady pace of change over time. The world turns, things change, and beliefs that once served you well will no longer be valid.

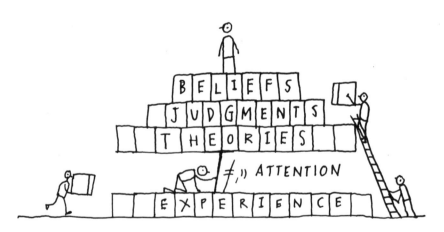

OUR STRUCTURES OF BELIEF
MUST EVOLVE CONTINUALLY IF WE
ARE TO STAY ON TOP OF THINGS

The novelist Robert Anton Wilson once wrote "All experience is a muddle, until we make a model." Liminal thinking is a way of intentionally disrupting your existing models by introducing more muddles. Mucking about with the muddles then can lead to new and interesting models that may work better than the models of the past.

Your beliefs can't evolve if you're not willing to introduce some chaos into the mix. To open new doors, you need to embrace that complexity. Liminal thinking is a way of navigating change by opening the door to ambiguity and uncertainty, recognizing that there can be no real creation without some destruction, a kind of urban renewal program for the mind.

EXERCISES

- Think about an area in your life that you'd like to see change. Consider the different paths and the different ways that change could end, both for others and for you. What are the risks? What might make those risks worth taking?

- Get a piece of paper and write a story about your future. What are the changes you would like to see? If you feel comfortable doing so, please share that story with me. I want to read it.

Evolve yourself.

If you can be open about how change affects you personally, you have a better chance of achieving your aims. To change the world, you must be willing to change yourself.

The heart has its reasons, of which reason knows nothing.

—Blaise Pascal

Now What?

Liminal thinking is something anyone can learn, but it's not easy. It's uncomfortable, even unsettling. It's a lot of work! Why would anyone want to do all these uncomfortable things, especially when it seems like the only rewards are increased ambiguity, uncertainty, and doubt?

The answer is this: Because it matters.

It matters because you matter. You owe it to yourself to be a whole, self-actualized person. It matters because your friends matter and your family matters. They deserve to be understood, even when they disagree. It matters because your work and your community matter. You owe it to them to be an important part of those communities, not just the people who agree with you.

It matters because the world matters.

Einstein was very concerned about the prospects for humankind in the Nuclear Age. He helped bring that world into being, so he felt responsible. He felt that substantial change in our thinking that would enable us to "abandon competition and secure cooperation" was necessary to secure our long-term survival.

He said, "A new type of thinking is essential if mankind is to survive and move toward higher levels."

That's the quote that I started this book with. I do believe that liminal thinking may be that type of thinking that Einstein was hoping for, a clear and viable way to secure the kind of cooperation that Einstein was seeking.

I have seen with my own eyes how liminal thinking can lead to dramatic effects in people's life and work, and I have shared some of those stories with you here.

Liminal thinking will enable you to become a positive force in the world, for yourself and for others, the kind of person who makes things better just by being there, and who leaves things better than you found them.

Don't think that you need to be the boss to bring these ideas to life. The leaders in an organization, or a family, or a nation, or any group, are not always the people at the top.

You can lead from anywhere, and I hope you do. I hope your journey is an exciting and joyful one, and I hope that one day you will tell me your stories. I look forward to hearing them.

—**Dave Gray**

For more information about liminal thinking, including tools and resources, and to send me a note or join our mailing list, please visit liminalthinking.com.

Appendix

Liminal Thinking Principles

1. **Beliefs are models.** Beliefs seem like perfect representations of the world, but, in fact, they are imperfect models for navigating a complex, multidimensional, unknowable reality.

2. **Beliefs are created.** Beliefs are constructed hierarchically, using theories and judgments, which are based on selected facts and personal, subjective experiences.

3. **Beliefs create a shared world.** Beliefs are the psychological material we use to co-create a shared world, so we can live, work, and do things together. Changing a shared world requires changing its underlying beliefs.

4. **Beliefs create blind spots.** Beliefs are tools for thinking and provide rules for action, but they can also create artificial constraints that blind you to valid possibilities.

5. **Beliefs defend themselves.** Beliefs are unconsciously defended by a bubble of self-sealing logic, which maintains them even when they are invalid, to protect personal identity and self-worth.

6. **Beliefs are tied to identity.** Governing beliefs, which form the basis for other beliefs, are the most difficult to change, because they are tied to personal identity and feelings of self-worth. You can't change your governing beliefs without changing yourself.

Liminal Thinking Practices

1. **Assume that you are not objective.** If you're part of the system you want to change, you're part of the problem.

2. **Empty your cup.** You can't learn new things without letting go of old things. Stop, look, and listen. Suspend judgment. What's going on?

3. **Create safe space.** If you don't understand the underlying need, nothing else matters. People will not share their innermost needs unless they feel safe, respected, and accepted for who they are.

4. **Triangulate and validate.** Look at situations from as many points of view as possible. Consider the possibility that seemingly different or contradictory beliefs may be valid. If something doesn't make sense to you, then you're missing something.

5. **Ask questions, make connections.** Try to understand people's hopes, dreams, and frustrations. Explore the social system and make connections to create new opportunities.

6. **Disrupt routines.** Many beliefs are embedded in habitual routines that run on autopilot. If a routine is a problem, disrupt the routine to create new possibilities.

7. **Act as if in the here and now.** You can test beliefs even if you don't believe they are true. All you need to do is act as if they were true and see what happens. If you find something that works, do more of it.

8. **Make sense with stories.** If you give people facts without a story, they will explain it within their existing belief system. The best way to promote a new or different belief is not with facts, but with a story.

9. **Evolve yourself.** If you can be open about how change affects you personally, you have a better chance of achieving your aims. To change the world, you must be willing to change yourself.

List of Character Traits

For use with the Johari window exercise. Get a printable copy of this list from http://xplaner.com/johariwindow.

Able	Absent-minded	Accepting
Adaptable	Attentive	Bold
Brave	Calm	Caring
Cautious	Charismatic	Cheerful
Clever	Creative	Compassionate
Complex	Confident	Crafty
Curious	Dependable	Determined
Dignified	Energetic	Extroverted
Focused	Friendly	Funny
Gentle	Giving	Hard-working
Happy	Helpful	Honest
Idealistic	Independent	Ingenious
Intelligent	Introverted	Kind
Knowledgeable	Logical	Loving
Mature	Modest	Nervous
Observant	Organized	Patient
Powerful	Proud	Quiet
Reflective	Relaxed	Religious
Responsive	Searching	Self-assertive
Self-conscious	Sensible	Sentimental
Shy	Silly	Spontaneous
Sympathetic	Tense	Trustworthy
Warm	Wise	Witty

Unpacking Beliefs

A worksheet for unpacking your beliefs.

1. Name the belief.

   I believe _____.
   YOUR BELIEF

2. Unpack the belief.

   I have _____, during which I noticed
   NAME YOUR EXPERIENCES
   that _____. Based on those observations,
   YOUR OBSERVATIONS
   I have a theory that _____, and I conclude
   DESCRIBE YOUR THEORY
   that _____. Therefore I believe _____.
   JUDGMENT   YOUR BELIEF

3. Now ask:

   - What other experiences might be possible or valid?

   - What might you not have noticed?

   - What other theories are conceivable?

   - What other conclusions might be reached?

   - What other beliefs might be valid?

The Roots of Liminal Thinking

Liminal thinking is a discipline with deep and tangled roots that are not easily unraveled. Many people practice liminal thinking intuitively, or learn it from a mentor, but up until now, this community has been a diffuse, distributed, disconnected population—a "community without a name." One of the goals of this book is to provide a name, a home, and a common language for that community.

The word *liminal* means a *state, stage,* or *period of transition*. It derives from the Latin root *limen*, which means *threshold*. This root appears in the following English words: preliminary (an event preceding something important), subliminal (below the threshold of consciousness), and lintel (literally threshold).

The first use of the word *liminal* in English was by James Sully, a psychologist, in 1884:

"Among these problems [of consciousness] is that of the limit, threshold, or liminal intensity. A certain degree of stimulation is necessary to a sense-impression: this is known as the liminal intensity."[1]

The concept of liminality as a state of transition was developed by the anthropologist Arnold van Gennep, in the early 1900s, in his book, *Le Rites de Passage* (*Rites of Passage*). The concept was further developed by another anthropologist, Victor Turner, in the 1960s.

Liminality has been described as "Betwixt and between...the period of margin...an interstructural situation."[2]

"Moments or periods of transition during which the normal limits to thought, self-understanding and behavior are relaxed, opening the way to novelty and imagination, construction and destruction."[3]

"Any 'betwixt and between' situation or object, any in-between place or moment, a state of suspense, a moment of freedom between two structured world-views or institutional arrangements. It relates to change in a single personality as well as social change and transition in large-scale settings...[it] opens the door to a world of contingency where events and meanings—indeed 'reality itself'—can be moulded and carried in different directions."[4]

Liminal thinking owes a great debt to Jainism and Buddhism, especially Zen Buddhism, the practice of mindful meditation, reflection on experience, and getting in touch with the reality of experience. Jainism is

1. James Scully, *Outlines of Psychology*, with Special Reference to the Theory of Education. A Textbook for Colleges (New York: Appleton and Company, 1884).
2. Victor W. Turner, "Betwixt and Between: The Liminal Period," in *Rites de Passage* (The Proceedings of the American Ethological Society, 1964).
3. Bjorn Thomassen, *Liminality and the Modern: Living Through the In-Between* (Farnham, UK: Ashgate Publishing, 2014).
4. Ibid.

also the source for the story of the blind men and the elephant, still the best parable for the nature of belief and reality that I know of.

Liminal thinking also owes homage to Socrates and Plato, especially Plato's metaphor of the cave.

One of the more important and more recent influences is that of the Pragmatists, a school of American philosophy founded by William James and Charles Sanders Peirce.

The Pragmatists, in turn, were a great influence on Alfred Korzybski, a Polish-American engineer who developed a "non-Aristotelian logic" that he called *general semantics* in the 1920s. Korzybski hoped that the adoption of general semantics would lead to an increase in sanity for the human race.

So far, Korzybski has not gotten his wish, but general semantics has influenced the development of a number of practical approaches that have been successfully applied in the field of psychotherapy, under the general category of systemic therapy, but specifically known as brief therapy, narrative therapy, solutions-focused therapy, and family therapy.

Some of the great thinkers in cybernetics and systems thinking were also strongly influenced by Korzybski and general semantics.

Another branch in the liminal thinking root system is the concept of nonviolent resistance, as practiced by Mohandas Gandhi and Martin Luther King, and nonviolent communication, a discipline inspired by nonviolent resistance and developed by Marshall Rosenberg.

Liminal thinking must also acknowledge a deep debt to organizational development, a discipline pioneered by Chris Argyris and his peers, specifically concepts like the ladder of influence (which I have described here as the pyramid of belief), self-sealing logic, and double-loop learning.

The scientific research program of neurophenomenology continues to supply a steady stream of new information that promises to provide insights for years to come.

Glossary

belief: A story in your head that serves as a recipe or rule for action.

bubble of belief or **belief bubble:** A defense mechanism that protects and reinforces existing beliefs by using self-sealing logic to deny the validity of alternative beliefs.

delight loop: A learning loop that creates a self-reinforcing spiral of positive behavior; also known as a *virtuous cycle*.

doom loop: A learning loop that creates a self-reinforcing spiral of negative behavior, often associated with distorted beliefs; also known as a *vicious cycle*.

double-loop learning: A way to get unstuck and escape doom loops by trying on new beliefs.

falsifiability: The possibility that a theory could be proven false. A theory is falsifiable if it is possible to conceive of an observation, experiment, or argument that would disprove it.

governing belief: A belief that is deeply tied to identity and feelings of self-worth, which serves as a foundation for other beliefs.

Johari window: A model for understanding your relationships, with yourself as well as others, developed by Joseph Luft and Harrington Ingham.

learning loop: A continuous feedback cycle of thinking and action, which creates habits of belief and behavior over time.

liminal thinking: The art of creating change by understanding, shaping, and reframing beliefs.

limiting belief: A belief that narrows the range of possibilities and may obscure valid opportunities.

neural coupling: A phenomenon characterized by people's brain patterns "mirroring" each other when they share stories.

priming effect: The tendency to focus on the things that will best meet your needs in any situation.

pyramid of belief or **belief pyramid:** The process by which we construct beliefs, based loosely on the Ladder of Inference by Chris Argyris.

safe space: An environment where people do not feel judged; where they feel comfortable enough to be vulnerable and reveal anxieties, frustrations, and emotional, unmet needs that they would otherwise conceal.

SCARF model: SCARF is an acronym that stands for Status, Certainty, Autonomy, Relatedness, and Fairness. The model was developed by David Rock of the Neuroleadership Institute.

self-sealing logic: Logic that is circular and self-validating. Self-sealing logic is impermeable to argument, because no evidence can be brought against it, no matter what.

single-loop learning: The process by which we translate needs into action, a continuous feedback loop that drives learning and improvement.

story prompts: Questions intended to explore people's experiences, and how they made meaning out of them.

story web: A shared world that is co-created by self-reinforcing, recurring behavior, as beliefs and actions interact over time. A story web is a version of reality: it may seem as if it is "just the way it is," but in fact it is only one of many possible realities.

strong inference: The intentional exploration of multiple, mutually contradictory hypotheses, in order to reduce bias and learn faster.

triangulation: The practice of developing multiple viewpoints and theories that you can compare, contrast, and combine to get a better understanding of what's going on.

Index

neural coupling, 124

Nokia, 45

O

objective reality, 5

objectivity, illusion of, 61–64

observation, resolving problems
through, 99–102

obviousness
baseline of reality and, 19
and belief system, 6–8

One Laptop per Child nonprofit, 67–68

organizational change, 75–77

Ortiz, Chris, 83, 85, 131

Our Stories project (Kochi), 67

P

paying attention and listening, 68–72

personal experience
needs based on, 24–25
separation from reality and, 4
as subset of reality, 14

Popper, Karl, 91

priming effect, 15

problems, resolving through
question asking, 99–102

pyramid of belief, 13, 16–19, 26

R

racism, 12

reality
concrete existence of, 6
confusion of beliefs with, 6
experiences as subset of, 14
objective, 5
separation of personal
experiences from, 4

subjective, 5
unknowable, 5

recurring doom loop, 105–112

Rising, Linda, 84–85

risk taking, 134–137

Roberts, Jason, 115–116

Rock, David, 79

routine, disrupting, 105–112

rumor and gossip, 81

S

safe space, 75–86

SCARF model (Status, Certainty,
Autonomy, Relatedness,
and Fairness), 79–80, 82

Seattle Post-Intelligence newspaper, 35

self-fulfilling prophecies, 90–91

self-sealing logic, 42–48, 53

self-worth, 52

shared assumptions, 44

single-loop learning, 117

Sipus, Mitchell, 99–102

solutions to needs, 99–102

Status, Certainty, Autonomy,
Relatedness, and Fairness
(SCARF) model, 79–80, 82

story prompts, 126–128

storytelling, 123–128

story web, 27, 29–31

subjective reality, 5

T

Taylor, Carolyn, 61

theories and judgments, 16–17

Toyota, 45–46

triangulation, 89–96

U

Uber, 51

unknowable reality, 5

W

weapons of mass destruction (Bush administration), 41–42

Wilson, Darren, 11

Wilson, Robert Anton, 139

Z

Zen practice (beginner's mind), 71–72

Zimmerman, Manfred, 14–15

Zuill, Woody, 109–110

Acknowledgments

I'd like to single out a few people for special mention. Lou Rosenfeld, my publisher, was supportive, courageous, and encouraging as this book dramatically shifted directions mid-course. The book's editor, Marta Justak, and compositor, Danielle Foster, have made the book a thousand times better. Additional thanks go to Heads of State—I love their cover design and am grateful for their patience. I'd like to single out researcher, author, and consultant Cynthia Kurtz for special mention. She spent many hours in careful review and thoughtful conversation, and she was instrumental in reframing the book from its original conception to something fundamentally different, and exponentially better than the book I started out to write. Most of the coda is borrowed from one of her emails. My wife, Michelle Milla, also spent many hours in dialogue and reflection that helped shape the book.

I am also grateful to the following people, who graciously shared their time and experiences, allowing me to interview them in the course of writing this book.

Adam Siemiginowski, Adam Yuret, Adrian Howard, Alan Dayley, Alex Ryan, Anna Curran, Annie Grace, Audrey del Rosario, Benno Schmidt, Bob Gower, Carlos Salum, Carolyn Taylor, Chris Ortiz, Christina Wodtke, Courtney Hemphill, Cynthia Kurtz, Dan Mezick, Dave Snowden, Desiree Sy, Despina Popadopoulous, Eleanor Vajzovic, Erica Kochi, Erik Martin, Esko Kilpi, Esko Reinikainen, Esther Derby, Eugen Oetringer, Glen Strachan, Jan Capps, Jeff Gothelf, Jeff Patton, Jeff Stevens, Jeffrey Eisenberg, Jeroen van Geel, Jessie Shternshus, Jill Willard, Jim Benson, Jon Jorgenson, Jurgen Appelo, Kate Otto, Kim Sykes, Kurt Hanks, Lane Halley, Leslie Hancock, Linda Rising,

Lisa Welchman, Madeline Gannon, Marc Rettig, Mark Knobil, Mark Oehlert, Mark Pierce, Markus Andrezak, Mathias Jakobsen, Melissa Perri, Michael Gold, Michael Margolis, Michelle Milla-Gray, Mick Calder, Mike Bonifer, Mitchell Sipus, Nikita Dyer, Nilofer Merchant, Patrick Scullin, Patrick van der Pijl, Pawel Brodzinski, Philip McKenzie, Ray Masters, Robert McCaa, Roy Adams, Sami Honkonen, Steve Denning, Teddy Ruge, Tonya McCarley, Trent Hone, Will Sansbury, and Woody Zuill.

About the Author

 DAVE GRAY is a leader and manager with a background in design. He has worked with many of the world's largest companies, as well as mid-sized businesses, start-ups, executives, and individuals.

He is the founder of XPLANE, a strategic design consultancy, and co-founder of Boardthing, a collaboration platform for distributed teams.

He has written two previous books on design, change, and innovation: *Gamestorming: A Playbook for Innovators, Rule-Breakers, and Changemakers* and *The Connected Company.*

His area of focus is the human element of change and innovation, specifically:

- What makes people embrace new ideas, especially when it involves changing deeply embedded habits and behaviors?

- How can you take plans, ideas, and strategies—things that sound like good ideas—and bring them to life, in the real world?

You can reach Dave by email at dave.gray@gmail.com.